Microteaching in Perspective

Microteaching in Perspective

Owen Hargie and Paul Maidment

Blackstaff Press
Ulster Polytechnic

40604

© Owen Hargie and Paul Maidment, 1979.

Published by Blackstaff Press Limited, 3 Galway Park, Dundonald, Co Down, BT16 8AN, and the Ulster Polytechnic, Jordanstown, Newtownabbey, Co Antrim.

ISBN 0 85640 158 7

Printed in Northern Ireland by Graphic Printing Services Ltd.

Contents

Preface   vii

1. The Development of Microteaching — A Review   1
   Owen Hargie

2. The Effectiveness of Microteaching — An Appraisal   15
   Owen Hargie

3. Surveys of Microteaching — A Comparative Account   28
   Paul Maidment

4. Microteaching in the British Isles — Part I of the Survey   42
   Paul Maidment

5. Microteaching in the British Isles — Part II of the Survey   51
   Paul Maidment

6. Problems, Plans and Microteaching Programmes   85
   Paul Maidment

7. Dimensions of Teaching Behaviour   95
   Owen Hargie

8. The Future of Microteaching   108
   Owen Hargie and Paul Maidment

Appendix 1A   115
Appendix 1B   116
Appendix 1C   117
Appendix 2   118
Questionnaire   123
Bibliography   128
Index   133

Acknowledgements

We would like to acknowledge Professor Roger Ellis who introduced micro-teaching at Ulster Polytechnic, and has since encouraged and fostered its development; our colleagues Dr George Brown of Nottingham University, and Ms Dorothy Whittington of Ulster Polytechnic, for their support and advice on many aspects of microteaching; Donald McIntyre of Stirling University who was kind enough to act as reader of manuscript for Ulster Polytechnic. We would like to thank all those members of staff at Ulster Polytechnic who have been involved in, and contributed to, the development of microteaching within the college. Also, we would like to express our great admiration to all those members of staff in other institutions providing courses of teacher training, who have participated in, and contributed to, the evolution of microteaching generally and to the survey we conducted in 1975 in particular. We wish especially to thank Dr Nigel Middleton without whose encouragement this book might never have been written.

Owen Hargie
Paul Maidment

Preface

This book comes at a time when several other titles have been published that are likewise concerned with the analysis of microteaching in teacher education. It has, we consider, a distinctive character in its being organised around a programme of investigation into the extent of microteaching, yet offering a number of perspectives on the subject. Its title is an inversion of the theme presented at the University of Liverpool Conference in 1974, 'Perspectives on Microteaching', an event that has proved influential in the development of microteaching in England and Wales.

Microteaching is a technique whereby trainees are introduced to the component skills of teaching, and are given an opportunity to practise these skills in scaled-down teaching encounters. Since this technique was introduced at Stanford University in 1963, it has generated a great deal of interest and has been the focus of many research investigations. Most of this research has shown microteaching to be effective in terms of improving the teaching performance of trainees, and also well-received in that the reactions of trainees to microteaching are usually favourable. (Hargie, 1977).

The first book to be written in this field, by Allen and Ryan (1969), presented microteaching as a new and exciting development in teacher education. At this time, research was at an early stage, and Allen and Ryan viewed their book as being, in many respects, both a motivation and a guide for future researchers. They pointed out future directions for such research, and outlined specific areas of microteaching which needed to be explored in more depth. While many of these areas have been investigated, there still remains a need for further exploration of many of the studies suggested by Allen and Ryan.

This present book, to be published a decade after the initial book by Allen and Ryan, is necessary for many reasons. Microteaching has progressed and evolved in many ways during the past ten years, and in many countries throughout the world. Surveys of microteaching have been conducted in the interim, in the USA, Australia, and Germany, and these surveys provide evidence· of the diversification of developments which have occurred. The initial Stanford 'model' of microteaching has been tried, tested and refined in many institutions of teacher training. At the same time, developments in teacher education have necessitated a re-evaluation of the role, and nature, of microteaching.

We have attempted in this book a presentation of the refinement, or at least the differentiation, of microteaching in teacher training. To further our knowledge of trends in microteaching, a comprehensive survey of all teacher training establishments in the UK was conducted. This survey, which is presented in chapters 4, 5 and 6, provided valuable data relating to the evolution of microteaching. When taken in conjunction with the surveys of microteaching conducted in other countries, as presented in chapter 3, this offers a very clear picture of the dissemination of this method. In particular, the analyses of specific components of microteaching, and of various approaches to the co-ordination of these components, should be of interest to the reader. Analysis of these surveys of microteaching forms one strand of our investigation of this technique contained in this text. A second strand incorporates an overview of microteaching, and developments therein, with an exploratory analysis of the future role of this technique. In many ways, we view microteaching as being at a crossroads. It has been found to be a successful training method and, as Perlberg (1976) pointed out, is now widely accepted and no longer an innovation. At the same time, there is no one accepted method of microteaching, since variations in the training format are many and varied. Thus while microteaching *per se* is not an innovation, many educationists working in this field still foresee valuable contributions to our knowledge and understanding of the process of teaching, emanating from within this framework (MacLeod and McIntyre 1977).

In chapter 1 we provide the reader with a review of the historical development of this technique, while chapter 2 outlines the research which has been conducted into determining its effectiveness. In both of these chapters, reference is made to research into specific components of microteaching, so that while this aspect is not covered in depth the reader is given useful sources to pursue. This approach has been adopted because this book is not intended as a research review, but rather research is regarded as one important feature within the entire spectrum of microteaching.

A similar approach is adopted to the study of microteaching within teacher education. A number of facets of teacher education are discussed briefly, with an emphasis being placed on how they will relate specifically to the microteaching format. We make no apologies for focussing on breadth rather than depth in many instances in this text, since as Allen and Ryan (1969) pointed out, microteaching has always been capable of '... opening entirely new avenues, perspectives, and alternatives to human exploration' (piii). Many of the avenues opened up by Allen and Ryan have since been explored and charted by other researchers in education. We would optimistically anticipate that at least some of the avenues we open up in this book will likewise be charted further by fellow educationists.

The third strand in our inquiry is one possible interpretation of the complexities of teaching, which attempts to incorporate teaching behaviour into an overall explanatory model for the process of classroom interaction. The theoretical perspectives examined in chapter 7 represent our tentative thoughts on the dimensions of teaching behaviour. These present perhaps the greatest challenge faced by proponents of microteaching — to somehow develop the reductionist strategy of analysing teaching behaviour, in order to account for more global, holistic teaching dimensions. Thus, although we regard this book as a new starting point, and a source of information for future research projects, we intend to put forward in subsequent work an exploration of certain avenues to which it points, notably the quality of school experience for pupils, rather as that for student teachers has been explored by researchers like Cope (1970) and Gallmeier and Poppleton (1978).

As the final strand, in Chapter 8, the future of microteaching is discussed, both within and without the UK. Again, our approach is one of discussing possible future directions, and of highlighting where more thought and effort will have to be devoted. We have offered a glimpse to the reader of the actual development of microteaching, and summarize its scale and significance before concluding in hopeful vein that microteaching is still developing both in focus and in format, and will, we believe, continue to do so for some considerable time. The controlled environment inherent in microteaching lends itself to scientific investigation, and, as a result, attracts enthusiastic researchers. It is therefore very likely '... that microteaching will continue to intrigue the imagination of people in the profession, and that it will indeed be a vehicle for unlocking new perspectives on the process of teaching and learning' (Allen and Ryan).

We consider our basic, if limited, objectives, to have been realized, in our description of 'the state of the art' of microteaching for the benefit of researchers and of tutors. We would express the desire that both pre-service and in-service teachers who will be participating in programmes of microteaching should be given an insight into the activity in which they will be engaged. We have found that trainees value a knowledge of the rationale for, and research into, microteaching. Once they understand what microteaching is all about, their commitment tends to increase. Furthermore, the provision to trainees of a theoretical structure for microteaching may well be a prerequisite for long-term retention of the teaching skills studied and practised (MacLeod and McIntyre, 1977). For these reasons, the notion that students 'do' micro-teaching, rather than 'study' microteaching may well be counter-productive. If students are unclear, or uncertain, about the rationale for, or validity of, microteaching then it would seem reasonable to expect that their overall commitment will be reduced accordingly.

We therefore present microteaching in the perspectives of the rationale for this technique, its historical development, its dissemination in several countries, research into its effectiveness, and possible theoretical structures which may contribute to an overall explanatory model for microteaching. We hope our approach may serve to whet the appetite of readers, to explore in more depth at least some of the issues which we raise. We are certainly optimistic about the future of microteaching, and the contributions which we believe can be made by this training method, to further knowledge of the processes of teaching and learning.

Ulster Polytechnic,
May, 1979.

Owen Hargie
Paul Maidment

References!—

Allen D. W., Ryan K.A., *Microteaching*. Addison-Wesley, 1969.

Cope, E., 'Teacher training and school practice'. *Educational Research*, 12 (1970) 2.

Gallmeier, T., Poppleton, P., 'A study of early school experience in the P.G.C.E. course at the University of Sheffield'. *British Journal of Teacher Education*, 4 (1978), 2, 125-35.

Hargie, O. D. W., 'The effectiveness of microteaching: A selective review'. *Educational Review*, 29 (1977) 2, 87-95.

MacLeod, G. R., McIntyre, D., 'Towards a model for microteaching' in D. McIntyre *et al* (eds) *Investigations of Microteaching*. Croom-Helm, London 1977.

Perlberg, A., 'Microteaching — present and future directions'. *Education Media International*, 2 (1976) 13-21.

The Development of Microteaching
A Review

Introduction

Microteaching began at Stanford University, California in 1963. At this time a number of educationalists at Stanford had decided that the existing techniques for training teachers 'how to teach' were far from satisfactory. The traditional method consisted of the 'sitting with Nellie' approach, whereby trainee teachers were sent out to schools to observe teachers in the classroom, with the implication being, as Stones and Morris (1972) point out, that the trainee should 'model the master teacher'. But this approach is beset by numerous problems and is far from satisfactory. One major problem is that it assumes that the teachers encountered by the trainees will be highly competent and worthy of note. However, since many teachers will not be highly competent, we are presented with the situation where trainees may either imitate teachers who leave a lot to be desired, or may end up having learned nothing from their period of observation. Furthermore the difficulties are increased in that quite often trainees are given no training in methods of observation prior to being sent into classrooms. (McAleese 1973).

The technique of modelling a master teacher would be acceptable if all teachers always displayed ideal teaching behaviours and were widely experienced teachers (McKnight 1971). Unfortunately, however, widely experienced and highly competent teachers are not available in sufficient numbers to cope with the demands of institutions of teacher training. Thus the technique of modelling the master teacher as a method of training student teachers how to teach is far from satisfactory. The question therefore arises as to what alternatives there are, and how this technique can be modified in order to make it more acceptable.

This, in fact, was the question which was being asked at Stanford. It was recognized that teaching is a very complex task, affected by a large number of variables, all of which may influence the behaviour of the participants and many of which are extremely difficult to cater for. The personality, sex, age, training, social background and previous experiences of the teacher will influence his classroom behaviour. Similarly the personalities, sex, age, social background and previous experiences of the pupils will affect their classroom behaviour. In addition the attitudes of the teacher and pupils to one another will affect any interaction between the two parties. Other variables in operation include the subject matter and its level of difficulty, the academic orientation and interest of both teacher and pupils, school location, headmaster's biases, community and economic factors and parental influence. All these factors are operative in the classroom situation and many of them will be interacting at any period of time. Morrison and McIntyre (1973) sum up this situation when they tell us that 'classroom behaviour is so complicated, occurs on so many levels, so rapidly, and with so many individuals that a representation of even a small part of the events is difficult'. (Page 27.)

As a result of the recognition of the many complexities involved in classroom teaching, the Stanford team felt that any attempt to train teachers could take place in a simplified situation. Attention was turned to other professions and an analysis of the training methods used indicated that in many cases complicated skills were taught by being 'broken down' into simpler skill areas, and also that such training often occurred in a simulated situation rather than in the real situation. Actors have always had their rehearsals, prior to the presentation of a play, when various scenes are practised in isolation until adjudged to be satisfactory. Similarly athletes and other sports players have always attempted to identify the crucial areas which affect performance and then practise these areas separately before 'putting them all together' when it matters most.

It was decided that if such an approach was adopted by teachers the results could be well worthwhile. The Stanford team therefore devised a programme of training which was composed of teaching a number of teaching skills in a scaled-down teaching encounter termed 'microteaching'. In microteaching the trainee taught a small group of between five and ten pupils for a short period of time (five to ten minutes) during which time he was to focus specifically on one particular skill of teaching, such as varying the stimulus. When the trainee finished his microlesson he received immediate feedback, usually in the form of tutorial guidance and in most cases in the form of a video replay of his 'teach', and again he focussed his attention on the particular skill in question. Each teaching skill was practised for two teaching sessions. The first practice session was given after the trainee had been informed as to what skill he was expected to learn, was given adequate training in the use of an observation schedule which measured these behaviours and was shown 'model' tapes of teachers using the behaviours in a teaching situation. This was referred to as the 'teach' of the skill. The trainee was then given the afore-mentioned tutorial and video feedback and was given some time to consider how he might improve his use of the skill (usually a minimum period of one hour). He then taught the same microlesson to a different group of pupils attempting to incorporate any improvements which he, or his tutor, believed would facilitate the development of the skill. This was known as the 'reteach' of the skill. Once again feedback was provided during which time the trainee could analyze what improvements had occurred.

This basically was the Stanford model of microteaching, consisting of the 'five r's' namely, 'recording, reviewing, responding, refining and redoing'. (Meier 1968). This technique had a number of advantages over the traditional teacher training methods of course lecture followed by classroom practice. Allen and Ryan (1969) outline five such advantages, namely:

1. the lessons are much shorter,
2. there are fewer pupils,
3. specific techniques can be studied closely,
4. most of the variables can be controlled,
5. more knowledge of results can be obtained.

Microteaching emphasized the notion of 'mastering the teaching model' rather than 'modelling the master teacher' (Stones and Morris 1972) and by so doing helped to solve some of the problems involved in teacher training. It provided the trainee with a safe, controlled environment in which to learn to identify and practise those skills which would be of value to him in the real situation. The emphasis was on the trainee learning to observe and analyze both his own teaching behaviour and the behaviour of other teachers.

The idea of scaling-down the teaching situation came before the notion of training the students in specific technical skills of teaching, and the observation schedule used was the Stanford Teacher Competence Appraisal Guide (STCAG). The emphasis was on global assessment of teaching performance in the 'micro' situation and microteaching was rather a 'microteaching practice situation'. However this emphasis did not prevail for long since the old problems which had plagued diagnosis and assessment of classroom practice were once again only too prevalent. By means of open discussion and common consent, rather than by any scientific research method, the team of educational researchers identified fourteen principal teaching skills, which they admitted would require the implementation of a number of research projects in order to refine or alter the list. The original skills were:-

1. Stimulus Variation
2. Set Induction
3. Closure
4. Nonverbal Behaviour
5. Reinforcement

6. Fluency in asking questions
7. Probing questions
8. Higher-order questions
9. Divergent questions
10. Recognizing attending behaviour
11. Illustration and use of examples
12. Lecturing
13. Planned repetition
14. Completeness of communication

(Allen and Ryan 1969)

This was the basic Stanford 'model' of microteaching and it was soon inaugurated at many American teacher training institutions and more gradually in Australia, Europe and many of the developing countries. However, while most institutions at first practised the original design in its exact form, many institutions became somewhat dissatisfied with this approach, finding it to be not entirely the best method for preparing their students. Rather than reject microteaching in its entirety, most of these institutions modified the original design to a greater or lesser degree. The reasons for these modifications can best be analysed by examining the component parts of microteaching and the responses to a number of surveys which have been conducted (see Chapter 3).

The Use of Pupils in Microteaching

Central to the concept of microteaching has been the notion of decreasing the number of pupils in the microlessons, and for the 'micro' element to be maintained it is usual for between five and ten pupils to be present. Many questions arise concerning the use of pupils. Firstly, what type of pupils should be used? Secondly, should pupils be paid for time in microteaching? Thirdly, should pupils be required to rate student teachers? Fourthly, should pupils participate in the feedback tutorials? Let us now look more closely at some of the issues raised by these questions.

In the initial stages in the development of microteaching at Stanford, the student teachers were required to teach a group of high-school pupils, if possible each of whom had been given a 'part' to play (such as 'slow-poke', 'know-it-all', 'couldn't care less' [Allen & Ryan 1969]). This demonstration lesson produced a large number of difficulties and was a complete failure. It was in fact destructive in that it often resulted in students breaking down into tears. The students found the situation unrealistic and as a result the notion of teaching role-playing pupils in a demonstration lesson was discarded in favour of teaching short lessons to non-role-playing pupils. These pupils were volunteers from local high schools, who were paid $1.00 per hour for time spent in microteaching, which took place outside normal school hours. Furthermore the pupils were trained in the use of rating instruments and were required to rate the student teachers. One important recommendation made by the Stanford researchers was that pupils used should be representative of pupils which the student teachers would later teach in schools.

Many colleges have modified this usage of pupils quite considerably. Some have replaced pupils in microteaching by peer groups of student teachers, largely because of the organizational problems involved when school pupils have to be recruited, and partly because of the expense involved, especially when large number of pupils have to be transported over fairly large distances. Indeed one study by Goldthwaite (1969) indicated that it was a valuable learning experience for peers, in terms of improving their own teaching performance, to participate as pupils in microteaching.

At Ulster College, however, we found that student teachers were most unhappy when teaching a peer group and indicated that they saw no relevance in such an exercise, finding it quite difficult in many instances to maintain any serious discussion in the microlessons. One notable exception to this general finding is with in-service further education teachers on the CNAA Certificate in Education course. These teachers attend college one day per week and spend sixteen afternoons in the Microteaching Unit, during which time they teach small peer groups. But this is in line with the Stanford suggestion since these teachers normally teach adults in colleges of further education and so the situation maintains a large degree of realism. For pre-service teachers however, pupils are obtained from neighbouring schools, and microteaching takes place during normal school hours. Ulster College arranges transport for the pupils to and from school and provides refreshments in the form of lemonade and biscuits which pupils receive during a mid-session break. Pupils are enlisted for a maximum of two hours per week, morning or afternoon, and are taken from a variety of primary, secondary or special care schools depending upon the requirements of the particular course.

A few studies have used pupil ratings of their teachers in order to ascertain how successful a certain course of training has been (Bush 1966; Fortune et al 1967; Wragg 1971). The findings suggest that pupil ratings can be of value, but few colleges actually employ pupils as raters, and here Ulster College is no exception. When this idea was floated at Ulster College it met with hostile reaction from both students and supervisors alike. One female BEd student commented, 'It's nerve-wrecking enough in front of the camera but if I thought those pupils were watching every move I made that would just finish me!' Apart from such apprehension on the part of trainees, there is also the fact that in microteaching the number of hours available is limited, and so to train pupils to become competent raters would not be a feasible proposition. Furthermore, we do not pay pupils for their time spent in microteaching and we feel that this makes for a more realistic setting. Pupils do learn from their microlessons and are usually enthusiastic about the experience, especially since we try to videotape the pupils at some time and replay this to them (as another form of positive reinforcement) usually in their early visits to the Microteaching Unit.

So far as it is possible to ascertain it would seem that no colleges use pupils in the actual tutorial and video-feedback phase of micro-teaching. This is chiefly because the presence of pupils in such a role could quite possibly 'finish' a few nervous students who would regard such an intervention as being a threat to their position. Also, given the above limitation, it is doubtful just what value such an exercise would have in terms of guidance to the student about his or her use of particular teaching skills. It would seem that such a venture would be beset by too many problems and the disadvantages appear to outweigh any advantages which might accrue, in a practical training programme. There would appear to be a case for involving pupils as sources of feedback either in research projects (see Chapter 2) or in a less formal manner (see Chapter 7).

Thus many modifications have taken place in terms of pupil participation in microteaching since the initial Stanford programme. At Ulster College we have found many advantages with the system used. The College is in a fortunate geographical location with many schools being situated within a very short distance. As a result little time is spent taking the pupils to and from college, and expense is kept at a minimum. Local schools are very enthusiastic about their pupils participating in microteaching and we have even had requests from principals to include their schools in our rota system. The facts that microteaching takes place during school hours, and that pupils are not paid make the exercise a much less mercenary affair. No pupil comes to the Unit for more than two hours every week for a maximum of fourteen weeks, and the time is far from wasted, as shall be illustrated later when discussing microlessons. Finally, it should be pointed out that at Ulster College the arrangements for microteaching pupils are administered by the same lecturer who is responsible for liaison with schools regarding teaching practice, and this ensures a consistent approach.

Microlessons

Another feature of microteaching is the notion of reducing the length of time spent actually teaching. This helps to reduce some of the complexity and gives the student teacher a greater opportunity to concentrate on the actual skills being trained, without having to worry too much about the subject matter involved. Usually the length of lessons in microteaching is between five and ten minutes — at Stanford the researchers found that five minutes was sufficient and that indeed length of lesson was not a major factor in skill learning.

At many colleges however, including Ulster College, the length of lesson has been increased gradually as the student progresses through his microteaching programme. At Ulster College we always begin the programme with a five minute teach which is at this stage quite sufficient. When practising most of the skills we operate a ten-minute teach, which the students find more rewarding. For the skills of 'set induction' and 'closure' we operate a fifteen-minute teach which gives the student a chance to present a topic at more length. As one tutor put it, 'How can you close a lesson which you have not taught, or open a lesson which you do not intend to teach!' — as would happen in a five-minute teach with these two skills.

We have found the notion of increasing lesson length gradually to be very helpful from the point of view of both student and tutor perceptions, making the whole exercise much more realistic for those involved. When all lessons in microteaching were kept to a five-minute time limit we were left with the criticism that we were not really preparing students for teaching practice. It was argued that while we were not throwing students in at the 'deep end', we were merely allowing them to paddle for a time and *then* proceeding to throw them in at the 'deep end'. As a result our present 'mini-teaching' programme is much more satisfactory in that students are gently led from the 'shallow end' into the 'deep end' while gaining experience at the various levels. (See Figure 1.1).

What we usually do is to 'integrate' the skills at certain levels and during this integration increase the lesson length (see table 1.1). This encourages the student to regard the skills as being interdependent variables rather than completely isolated pieces of behaviour. It also means that the morning or afternoon spent in microteaching can provide a useful learning experience for the pupils involved, who will experience three or four 15-25 minute teaches in the course of the programme each week during the latter weeks. Quite often two students will share a common theme and one will proceed where the first has left off, making the exercise even more valuable for the pupils. Furthermore, students are required to teach lessons in their own subject area and are given advice from subject tutors as to which material lends itself to the teaching skill or skills being practised. This makes microteaching seem a more valid exercise for students who are invariably worried about how to teach their subject matter in schools. The emphasis is always on the student's use of the teaching skills, but often remarks will be made in tutorials as to how the use of the skills could be improved by altering the subject matter.

Thus at Ulster College, and at many other colleges, microteaching now serves the dual role of training students in the use of teaching skills and also preparing students to teach longer lessons in their own subject area. The maximum time for lessons in microteaching at Ulster College is twenty-five minutes, and we find that this is a satisfactory time limit at the end of a

FIGURE 1.1
A COMPARISON OF THE TWO APPROACHES

A. THE MINI-TEACHING PROGRAMME

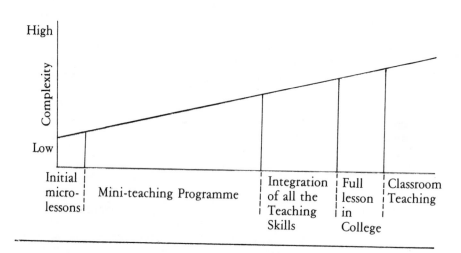

B. THE TRADITIONAL MICROTEACHING PROGRAMME

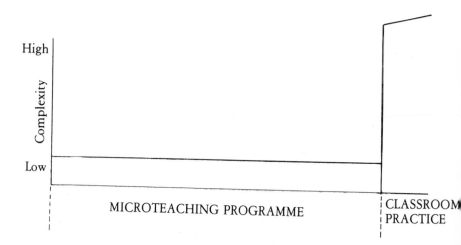

TABLE 1.1

TYPICAL MICROTEACHING PROGRAMME

Week	Activity	
1	Introduction to Microteaching	
2	Pre-Tape	5 minute teach
3	Questioning	10 minute teach
4	Reinforcement	10 minute teach
5	Integration of Questioning and Reinforcement	10 minute teach
6	Stimulus Variation	10 minute teach
7	Integration of Questioning, Reinforcement and Stimulus Variation	15 minute teach
8	Explanation	10 minute teach
9	Illustration and use of Example	10 minute teach
10	Integration of activities in weeks 3, 4, 6, 8 & 9	15 minute teach
11	Set Induction	15 minute teach
12	Closure	15 minute teach
13*	Integration of all skills	25 minute teach
14	Tutorials for week 13	NO TEACH
15	Remedial	10 minute teach
16	Post-Tape. Comparison of pre- and post-tape	10 minute teach

* No tutorials on week 13 owing to length of teaches. Tutorials to take place on week 14.

microteaching programme both in terms of time-tabling and in terms of student learning in relation to integration of skills. This approach seems to us to be an improvement on the Stanford model in preparing students for teaching practice in the classroom. A long programme comprising a large number of short teaches may in theory appear to be a good technique, but in practice the students become frustrated with 'bitty lessons' and their early enthusiasm often wanes in the later stages. With the gradation in lesson length we have found that student interest is maintained at a high level throughout without apparently affecting skill learning adversely, as measured by supervisory ratings. Students also regard this as a more valid preparation for teaching practice, and their level of confidence is thereby increased.

Feedback Tutorials

One of the most controversial features in the development of microteaching has been the organization and format of the feedback tutorials. Basically there are three variations possible in relation to feedback tutorials, namely:-

1. Tutorial feedback only. Here the student teacher receives feedback from an experienced tutor but does not have his performance recorded on tape.
2. Audio-visual feedback only. Here the student teacher receives feedback in the form of a replay of his lesson on a video-recorder but does not receive any tutorial advice.
3. Tutorial and audio-visual feedback. This is a combination of the previous alternatives. The student and tutor will view a video recording of the students lesson and the tutor will offer advice and constructive criticism.

While these are the three basic forms of feedback available there are of course other variations within some or all of these. Students may receive individual tutorials or they may have group tutorials with a number of peers (this applies to all three modes above). Feedback may be immediate or may be delayed for anything between one hour to one week. Furthermore, feedback may also be given in the form of counts or ratings on observation schedules. Indeed there is evidence to suggest that without such additional information, changes in teaching performance may only be minimal (James 1970) and that without observation instruments most spontaneous observations are related to self image (Waimon and Ramseyer 1970). In addition it may be the case that students are assessed on their performance in microteaching and such a factor may greatly influence the nature and efficiency of feedback. There are some tentative findings to suggest that students do prefer to be assessed in microteaching (Hargie 1977) and so this factor may also be related to student attitude to microteaching.

These are but a few of the possible variations in relation to the feedback phase of microteaching. Unfortunately, there are few concrete conclusions to be drawn since, despite the fact that a great deal of work has been published in the field of microteaching, comparatively little attention has been paid to the process of self-viewing (MacLeod 1973; Brusling 1972), possible variations in the use of audio-visual feedback (Griffiths 1972) and to the use of tutors (Griffiths 1973; McAleese and Unwin 1971; Olivero 1970).

Some research has been conducted relating to the value of tutorial guidance in microteaching with the general finding being that, while the presence of a tutor does not always affect students' teaching behaviour, students do prefer to have a tutor present [(Perrott (1972); Gregory (1971); McIntyre (1971); McIntyre and Duthie (1974) Tuckman and Oliver (1968); Kieviet (1972)]. On the other hand some researchers have found that tutors are effective in relation to changes in teaching behaviour of students in microteaching [McKnight (1971); Orme (1966); McDonald and Allen (1967); Olivero (1965)]. These seemingly contradictory findings are explained by Griffiths (1974) as being due to the fact that supervisory effectiveness is linked to other aspects of the situation. Factors which may be operative here include the overall organization of the microteaching programme, the level of competence of the student, the expectations of the students regarding supervisory behaviour and the type of feedback provided by supervisors.

An analysis of the research evidence indicates the importance of training students to identify and discriminate the teaching skills involved (Wagner 1973). It would appear that in a highly organized microteaching framework, where students are presented with model tapes in linked theory lectures, students can demonstrate a high level of skill competence and the role of the tutor becomes a supportive rather than instructive one. On the other hand, in a less well organized microteaching framework quite often students will approach the practical element with a low level of skill competence; in such a context the role of the tutor becomes an instructive one, since discrimination learning is still taking place at this stage. (See Chapter 2 for a more detailed discussion). Thus the efficacy of the tutor in microteaching depends on the structure of the skills training programme itself, but few researchers would suggest that tutors should be dispensed with altogether. Rather it would seem that their role will vary from one situation to another and that this fact should be catered for in the planning and implementation of a microteaching programme.

At Ulster College, tutors are used in both supportive and advisory roles. With the linkage between subject matter and skill training being a prominent one, tutors are utilized to advise students about choice of subject matter in relation to skill or skills being trained, length of microlessons and ability of pupils. This is a most important function, since in most cases microteaching occurs with first year pre-service teachers who have had no experience of lesson planning. The supportive role occurs in feedback tutorials when students need guidance as to their teaching performance and appreciate constructive criticism from an experienced source. Although in most instances skill learning does not occur at this particular stage, it is important for the students to have a tutor present, and this seemingly increases the face validity of the exercise. One other advantage is that, where microteaching tutors act as supervisors on teaching practice, the exchange of comments in the simulated environment serves as an induction to practical teaching visits.

Teaching Skills

The rationale of breaking the teaching act down into smaller component skills is allied to the concept of microteaching. As we have already said, researchers at Stanford developed a list of fourteen teaching skills on a fairly ad hoc basis with the recommendation being that these could then be altered or refined by subsequent research findings. Following this recommendation there was a vast amount of research work carried out, with a fair proportion relating to the use of teaching skills both in the microteaching and classroom contexts [(Shepardson (1972; Wright and Nuthall (1970); Perkins (1965); Ahlbrand (1972); Kremer and Perlberg (1971); Rosenfield (1972); Delefes and Jackson (1972).]

Barak Rosenshine (1971) examined the relationships between a number of teaching behaviours and student achievement. He focussed on teaching skills such as reinforcement, explanation, questioning and stimulus variation, giving a detailed analysis of some of the research which had been carried out in these areas. The results of this review suggested that the use of these skills by teachers facilitates higher student achievement. In another similar study Rosenshine and Furst (1971) reviewed some fifty studies, in which they claimed to identify eleven teacher behaviour variables which showed great promise in relation to student achievement.

However, in a detailed re-examination of these studies, Heath and Nielson (1974) discovered a number of features which they found disturbing. Firstly, they argued, operational definitions of teacher behaviour that have little in common were often combined by Rosenshine and Furst as examples of a single teaching variable. Secondly, they claimed, operational definitions of teaching used in the review by Rosenshine and Furst did not always relate to the teaching variables under which they were included. Thirdly, it is argued, these operational definitions were defined so vaguely as to be of little value in the training of teachers. Heath and Nielson also pointed out that two other important variables were ignored, namely the content of the lessons in the various studies, and the age, background and ability of the students being taught.

Certainly Heath and Nielson highlighted some glaring errors in the Rosenshine and Furst study. It does seem that some of the teaching 'behaviours' are rather large to be regarded as isolated (eg. 'task-orientated and/or business-like behaviours'), and here we would agree with Heath and Nielson. However to conclude from this that: '... the effects of techniques of teaching on achievement ... are likely to be inherently trivial...' (p.484) is to take a very extreme viewpoint. This in fact is equivalent to saying that teachers are of little value, since if their influence is trivial there must be little necessity for them at all. Yet Heath and Nielson fail to suggest any viable alternatives!

What would seem to be the case is that not enough concentrated research has been conducted in order to ascertain exactly which teaching behaviours are effective, and in what respects, with which group of pupils, in relation to what subject matter. However, in recent years a number of researchers have begun to investigate these various areas and the outlook is very bright indeed. (Wyckoff 1973). Since the introduction of microteaching this research has taken on a more systematic approach, away from the global teaching areas such as 'teacher warmth', towards smaller skill areas such as 'redirection of teacher questions'. This has enabled researchers to be more objective in the collection of data, and more confident in the relevance of their findings. At the same time, this is not to say that teaching dimensions, such as warmth, cannot be catered for within a microteaching programme. (This aspect is discussed in Chapter 7).

A good example of the skills approach has been the Teaching Skills Development Project (TSDP) which was initiated in 1972 at the Department of Education of the University of Sydney. This TSDP represents a concerted attempt to provide a scientific basis for the analysis of teaching. Again the emphasis is on the development of 'micro-criteria' for teacher effectiveness, resulting in a skills-based programme for teacher training. Already the team involved in the TSDP has produced a comprehensive review of the relevant research findings relating to a number of the technical skills of teaching (Turney et al 1973, 1975). As a result of this work they have developed teaching programmes for each of the skills, with a firm grounding in the research findings, and a practical application in an accompanying microteaching format. Furthermore, their outlook is a most realistic one and they have devised the TSDP with an emphasis on flexibility. Teacher educators are not expected to adhere rigidly to the structure of the various courses, but are encouraged to mould the framework to suit their particular needs. The skills presented in the TSDP are fairly representative of other work in the field and include:-

1. Reinforcement
2. Questioning
3. Variability
4. Explanation
5. Set Induction

6. Closure
7. Discipline and Classroom Management
8. Small Group and Individualized Teaching Skills
9. Skills relating to the Development of Discovery Learning and Creativity in Pupils.

These are the teaching skills which seem to be central in most microteaching programmes. There are variations both within and without this list. A need exists for each institution which has introduced a programme of microteaching to refine and further develop the identifiable component skills of teaching in order to meet their own requirements (Cooper 1967). At Ulster College, for example, we have developed the skill of 'demonstration' which is important to teachers in the fields of craft, home economics and physical education but does not figure in either the Stanford or Sydney packages (although elements of this skill are contained in 'Illustration and Use of Example'). Another illustration would be the fact that the teaching behaviours operative in the skill of classroom management will vary between, for example, teachers of educationally retarded children and teachers in further education.

Conclusion

These are factors which must be borne in mind when planning a microteaching programme — an exercise which requires considerable thought and effort (Brown 1975). The result has been a wide diversification in microteaching programmes with most teacher training establishments adapting this technique to best cater for the needs of their students. In addition there often has to be a compromise between what each institution would regard as an ideal programme and the practicalities of the situation. Thus consideration must be given to the finances available, the possibility of obtaining pupils from neighbouring schools, the time allocated to microteaching, the presence and training of tutorial staff and the relevant teaching skills.

The term 'microteaching' now covers a variety of usages, many of them scarcely recognizable when compared with the original Stanford model. Some elements are central to the concept of microteaching and as such should be a prerequisite for anyone planning to implement this procedure. If microteaching is to be 'micro', there must be a reduction in the complexity of the teaching situation, in the form of shorter lessons, fewer pupils and a concentrated focus on a small number of teaching skills at some stage. These need not all be operative throughout a microteaching programme, but if they are all absent then surely to entitle such a training programme 'microteaching' must be to use a misnomer.

The Effectiveness of Microteaching
An Appraisal

Introduction

One of the most controversial, yet most widely accepted, areas in teacher education has been the practical teaching component. Student teachers, as part of their training programme, are required to spend a fairly large proportion of their time either teaching in schools, or observing qualified teachers at work in the classroom. The rationale for this system is a fairly obvious one: since the trainees intend to become teachers, let them see other teachers at work and, further, give them the opportunity to teach. The trainees must be given some form of feedback as to their teaching performance. This usually takes the form of supervisory consultation, whereby a supervisor from the college concerned visits the school at which the student is based, observes a lesson and then confers with the student as to his or her performance (Cohen 1969).

Many problems arise here. There will be individual differences between supervisors with respect to observation abilities and type of feedback given. In addition there is the possibility of the supervisor visiting the student during his best lessons and thereby obtaining a misleading impression of teaching prowess. Other factors which may be operative include the time of day, academic level of the pupils, type of school and the subject matter being taught (Collier 1959). For all of these reasons, there seems to be a large element of chance involved in the practical training and assessment of teachers during their period of 'apprenticeship' (Dent 1971). With regard to the effectiveness of practical teaching, this is difficult to assess. The problems faced with respect to any large-scale examination of teaching practice are enormous. This would involve a large team of researchers, travelling wide distances, over a long period of time, before any conclusions could be reached. It would be a very expensive venture indeed. Perhaps, however, a cost analysis of teaching practice could be calculated in a method similar to that adopted by Kennedy (1975) for microteaching.

Alternatives

One possible method of increasing the overall effectiveness of teaching practice, while reducing the financial expenditure, would be to involve teachers in schools in the practical assessment of teacher training. This, of course, would necessitate the training, and presumably paying, of the teachers concerned. It would, however, ease the burden on colleges, by greatly reducing the amount of travelling currently being undertaken by supervisors (Emmet 1965). This could also be achieved by arranging with trainees and schools to have lessons video-recorded in schools and sent to the college to be analysed by supervisors. Feedback could be conveyed to the trainee in a number of ways; namely, by telephone conversation, by returning the tape along with written comments which the trainee could read while viewing his performance on videotape; or by a conference between trainee and supervisor in the college at a later date. These feedback components could, of course, be combined.

Other approaches which have been introduced include the 'practice school' and/or 'team teaching' methods (Price 1964; Coltham 1966) as well as 'group practice' (Kirwin and Shaw 1966). All these techniques have the advantage of reducing the expenditure involved in practical teaching, while increasing the feedback given to trainees. It is not our intention in this book to discuss these alternatives in detail, but rather to illustrate that such techniques are possible.

One other method which has been introduced into practical teaching programmes, namely microteaching, has proved to be extremely popular. Few educationists would however regard it as a replacement for teaching practice. Because microteaching is a scaled-down teaching encounter, which takes place in a controlled environment, it lends itself to scientific analysis and has generated a large amount of research material. Whether microteaching is to be regarded as an alternative, or as complementary, to teaching practice, the question must first be asked 'Just how effective is it?' It is on this question we now focus our attention, by examining the research material which has been produced.

The Effectiveness of Microteaching

Most of the criticisms which have been levelled at the microteaching framework have related to the conceptual basis for the skills approach to teacher training (Spelman and St. John Brooks 1973; Beattie 1972; Smith 1967). There is little research evidence to support such criticisms, since most studies which have been conducted in this area have tended to report findings which support the microteaching format. The rationale behind the microteaching technique is that the trainee teacher is led gently into the teaching situation; rather than being thrown into the deep end in the classroom, in the hope that he will manage somehow despite having had no prior practice opportunities. The ultimate criterion, to continue the analogy, will be the number of good 'classroom swimmers' who emerge from each pool, and for microteaching to be of value it should produce at least as many as the traditional technique produced.

One indication of the total amount of research which has been published in relation to microteaching is the fact that while a comprehensive bibliography of microteaching was published by McAleese and Unwin (1973), only two years later Falus and McAleese (1975) found it necessary to publish another bibliography covering the intervening years. A fair proportion of this work has dealt with an attempt to ascertain just how successful microteaching really is. In order to do so the researchers involved have used four main criteria for measuring 'success' namely:-

1. Actual teaching performance
2. Pupil attitudes to their teacher
3. Trainee teachers' attitudes to their course of training
4. Increases in pupil learning.

While the last of these, increases in pupil learning, is the best measure of successful teaching, the other three criteria are also useful as indicators of just how beneficial the training procedure used has been, and for this reason we believe they can be of benefit in any assessment of the value of microteaching in teacher education.

1. *Actual Teaching Performance*
Undoubtedly the most common criterion has been the analysis of changes in teaching performance as a result of microteaching measured either by ratings of behaviour or actual counts of behaviour. In some cases no control group is used and a comparison of pre- and post-treatment tests of teaching performance is employed, while in other cases an Experimental Group who have received microteaching is compared to a Control Group who have received the traditional training methods.

Allen (1972) compared twelve male college seniors who had received microteaching with a group of thirteen similar students who had been trained by traditional methods. He found that microteaching was more effective for improving trainee performance in the use of stimulus variation, reinforcement, developing main points, probing and closure, as measured by ratings of performance. Similarly Kissock (1971) found that microteaching significantly increased trainee teachers' use of higher order questioning, as compared to a control group of trainees who were given training in the use of this skill in the form of being shown 'model' tapes and told how to use higher order questions in the classroom. (p<0.01). However, in a retention test four weeks after the post-test, Kissock found no difference between the groups, indicating the importance of the discrimination learning element in the Control Group treatment. This result seems to suggest that while the practical teaching element of microteaching may work as a means whereby a student can demonstrate what he has learned, it is not a vehicle for learning the skill itself.

This fact is borne out by Wagner (1973) who found that a group of students at the University of Michigan who received discrimination training in the use of pupil-centred teaching behaviour were more effective than a group of students who received the practical teaching and feedback elements of microteaching but no discrimination training. Further it was found that this latter group did not differ significantly from a control group of students who received no treatment whatsoever. Wagner suggests that where experimenters have found microteaching to be effective, it may be that it was the discrimination training which caused the change in behaviour rather than the actual practice of microteaching. Indeed this would also explain the results obtained by Peterson (1973), who found no difference between two groups of students in their use of questions, one of which received microteaching while the other did not. Upon closer examination it transpires that indeed both groups did undergo discrimination training in the skill of questioning and that one group was given the opportunity to practise while the other was not.

In yet another study of this nature Goldthwaite (1969) compared three groups of ten students. Group A taught a number of lessons to peers in microteaching; Group B acted as the micro-class for these lessons, while Group C did not participate in microteaching. Students were rated by supervisors during student teaching practice, and it was found that Group B had actually benefited more from microteaching than had Group A, while both groups improved in their performance more than Group C. One possible reason for this result may be that the members of Group B were required to critique the performance of Group A members during microteaching and evaluate it on a Demonstration Evaluation Form. As a result their discrimination learning of the required behaviour was probably heightened, and was superior to that of Group A members who were not required to analyse the skill so closely.

Kallenbach and Gall (1969) carried out a study in which a group of nineteen students at San Jose State College Education Department were placed in a microteaching group, while a similar group of eighteen students were placed in a Student Teaching (ST) group. Both groups were given discrimination training in the use of specific teaching skills, and were required to teach a five-minute lesson before and after the training programmes.

One group received microteaching while the other group received the traditional ST training methods. All students were rated on the Stanford Teacher Competence Appraisal Guide (STCAG) and the Instrument for the Observation of Teachers Activities (IOTA). It was found that the two experimental groups did not differ from each other on any of the post-training ratings of teacher effectiveness, although the authors conclude that microteaching is a superior training strategy since it achieves similar results when compared with traditional training methods in only one-fifth the time. However, the authors fail to take into account the fact that both groups did receive discrimination training in the use of teaching skills — a technique which developed with microteaching.

The effects of video feedback were analysed in a study by Waimon and Ramseyer (1970) who compared various methods of presenting this feedback. They utilized four groups of ten students, and each group received feedback in one of four forms:-

1. Supervisory Control Group. Supervisory feedback but no audio-visual feedback.
2. Video Group One (Child). Audio-visual feedback with the camera focussed only on the pupils. No supervisory feedback.
3. Video Group Two (Child-Teacher). Audio-visual feedback with the camera focussed on a side-view of teacher and pupils. No supervisory feedback.
4. Video Group Three (Teacher). Audio-visual feedback with the camera focussed on the teacher alone. No supervisory feedback.

All students received discrimination training, and were required to complete a modified version of STCAG for one filmed lesson. In addition four supervisors rated the lesson and the means of their ratings were compared with the students' ratings. No differences were found between any of the groups studied and this would seem to indicate once again the importance of the discrimination training involved.

The results of these studies appear to suggest that perhaps the practice element of microteaching should be eliminated and more emphasis placed on the ability of trainees to discriminate the relevant behaviours being trained. It should be remembered, however, that the component skills approach is vital to discrimination learning as well as to microteaching and that all these elements developed in the same process and have in fact now merged into the technique of microteaching which includes the modelling of teacher behaviours, the opportunity to practise these behaviours and the provision of feedback with regard to performance. Microteaching offers trainees a safe practice environment in which they can encounter some of the problems they will later face in the real situation, and allows them to interact with pupils of the same age group that they will eventually be dealing with. Furthermore the advantages of self-confrontation should also be emphasized (Fuller and Manning 1973). This type of video feedback, when properly controlled, encourages a critical self-awareness on the part of trainees which might otherwise be difficult to achieve.

For these reasons we would argue that while much consideration should be given to the discrimination learning component of microteaching, the opportunity for trainees to practise should also be included, while at the same time more research should be conducted into various means by which this practice opportunity can be made more valuable in terms of skill learning.

An analysis of this research seems to indicate that discrimination learning is a critical feature in the training of skilled performance in teaching. This raises some pertinent questions about the relevance of classroom practice in teacher education. The inference here is that if the practical component of microteaching does not appear to have a critical role in the performance of trainees, then perhaps the practical component of classroom practice is in a similar position.

To continue the analogy, it could be argued that on the basis of the findings in microteaching, classroom practice will not affect the behaviour of student teachers. It should be sufficient for the trainees to be given discrimination training with regard to teaching in the classroom by being taught what exactly the central features involved are, and learning to identify these. Trainees could then be given periods of classroom observation, as opposed to practice, in order to sample the 'real' situation.

This, however, would be to take an extreme viewpoint. It assumes that all of the central features of classroom teaching can be identified and discriminated, and this is a very large assumption. In practical teaching, as in microteaching, it can be argued that the trainee is learning a problem-solving approach which will enable him to generalize from one situation to another (see Chapter 7). Whether such a factor could be taught by discrimination training is doubtful. In addition, the attitude, confidence and motivation of the trainee will be affected by practice. Students value such practice, and so from the point of view of face validity, periods of classroom practice are probably essential in teacher training.

This is not to say that approaches to teaching practice have always been satisfactory. More research needs to be conducted in order to ascertain exactly what the trainee learns from his periods of classroom teaching. Once we have discovered more about this, it is likely that certain elements of this learning will be capable of being imparted to trainees by methods other than classroom practice. To a certain extent this process has already begun, as the review of some of the research which has been carried out in relation to microteaching has indicated.

A number of other studies have indicated the effectiveness of microteaching. Davis (1970) compared a control group of students who received no microteaching with an experimental group which participated in microteaching just prior to student teaching. The focus was on the skill of set induction. Davis made videotapes of both groups' presentations in the classrooms of selected public schools in North Carolina, and had these tapes rated by a panel of three educators in relation to the student teachers use of the skill of set induction. He found that the microteaching group achieved higher scores than did the control group, indicating that the programme of microteaching had been of value.

Jensen and Young (1972) found that students who had received microteaching received significantly higher ratings on five factors extracted from the Sinba Teacher Performance Evaluation Scale, than did a control group of similar students who received no microteaching whatsoever. The five factors were:-

1. Personality traits
2. Warmth of teacher behaviour
3. General classroom atmosphere
4. Lesson usefulness
5. Teacher interest in pupils.

Both groups were studied three times while on classroom practice and it was found that the microteaching group did not show significant superiority until the second or third rating, and the authors suggest that this may be because the subjects learned a basic problem-solving attitude during microteaching which is progressively related to teaching performance. That this problem-solving skill is likely to be task- or lesson-orientated as opposed to pupil-centred, is demonstrated by the fact that the microteaching group did not differ significantly from the control group in a sixth factor, namely teacher interest in pupil achievement, and also by the fact that in Factor 5 the control group performed better on the first two ratings. This seems to suggest that any programme of microteaching should lay greater emphasis on those skills which aim at increasing pupil participation in the lesson.

In an experiment at the University of Exeter, Wragg (1971) had four groups of students (four in each group) teach a ten minute lesson to a group of ten children, and one hour later teach the same lesson to a different group of children. In between each of the groups received a different type of feedback:

Group 1 received feedback from television and from Flanders Interaction Analysis Category system (FIAC).

Group 2 received feedback from television alone.

Group 3 received feedback from FIAC alone.

Group 4 received no feedback.

No tutorial feedback was given to any group, and FIAC feedback was provided in the form of percentage totals of each category used. The results of this study indicated that students from Group 1 were most successful in terms of increasing pupil talk and decreasing the amount of lecture, and that students from Groups 2 and 3 were more successful than Group 4 in achieving similar results. These results support the microteaching format in that they indicate that feedback from television and from measuring instrument is more effective than feedback from only one of these sources alone, which in turn is more effective than no feedback whatsoever.

Fortune et al (1967) reported on work carried out at Stanford University with 140 pre-service teachers. All of these students underwent tests of performance before and after a six week period of microteaching. The results of these tests indicated that nine of the first twelve items on STCAG showed a significant mean gain over the six weeks ($p < 0.01$) indicating substantial improvement on the students use of these items. The authors pointed out that this finding was in accordance with the findings of the 1963 and 1964 Stanford Summer Microteaching Clinics, both of which also affirmed the effectiveness of microteaching. Indeed Bush (1966) confirms these results when he tells us that in the 1963 Stanford Clinic the microteaching group performed at a higher level of competence than did a traditionally trained group, despite the fact that they spent only ten hours per week in microteaching as compared with twenty to twenty-five hours per week spent in the traditional teaching.

Another study which indicated the effectiveness of microteaching was that of Britton and Leith (1971). They divided fifty-six first year College of Education students into two random groups of twenty-eight students. One of these groups received a course of twenty hours training in microteaching while the other group acted as a control and continued with their normal studies. The microteaching group practised the skill of set induction. After the treatment all students were placed on teaching practice and rated by tutors on a 7-point scale. On the basis of these ratings students were divided into three categories namely 'Good', 'Average' and 'Poor'. Results indicated that microteaching had the effect of reducing the number of 'weak' students and increasing the number achieving a 'good' grade, as compared to the control group. Britton and Leith therefore concluded that microteaching had had a beneficial effect. Brown (1968) carried out an experiment at Wayne State University in which forty-eight students were randomly divided into four treatment groups, three of which received microteaching while the remainder did not. All students were rated pre- and post-treatment on the six performance items of STCAG and it was found that while the microteaching group received significant gains on five of these six items, the control group achieved a significant gain on only one of these six items, as measured by a group of three independent raters. Once again this would seem to indicate that indeed microteaching is an effective teacher training programme.

Perrott et al (1975) tested a self-instructional microteaching course on the skill of 'Effective Questioning' by monitoring the changes in the teaching behaviour of twenty-eight in-service teachers who took part in the course. The training programme consisted of one three hour session at Lancaster University each week for a total of five weeks during which time they studied preparatory material, viewed instructional video-tapes, taught a ten-minute microlesson to a group of five pupils, analysed this teach and then did a re-teach of the lesson to a different group of five pupils with a further analysis (both on video and using self-evaluation forms). The twenty-eight teachers (14 M; 14 F) were tested immediately before, immediately after, and again four months after microteaching. Results of these tests indicated that the microteaching programme had been successful in that significant changes were recorded in eight out of fourteen behaviours being trained.

A number of other studies have also found microteaching to be successful. Nuthall (1972) found that students who received microteaching training in the use of questions used this skill to a greater extent than did a control group who received no such training. Kremer and Perlberg (1971) found that students trained in the use of higher order learner questions increased both the number and quality of such questions after a programme of microteaching and received higher ratings of performance as measured by two independent raters. Kieviet (1972) found that teachers trained in the use of FIAC and given a programme of microteaching improved significantly on five of seven selected variables, namely teacher/pupil talk; lecturing/asking questions; lecturing/total; extended pupil talk/total and the indirect/direct teaching ratio.

These studies are fairly representative of the type of research which has been conducted in this field, and all of them seem to indicate the effectiveness of microteaching in relation to improvement in teaching performance. Having ascertained that the technique is successful it would seem that in future, research in this area will concentrate more specifically on certain components of microteaching such as effects of various types of feedback, of various observation schedules, of various types of 'models', of various skill combination and so on. Indeed to date a number of researchers have carried out work in some of these areas (Clift et al 1976; Brusling 1972; McIntyre 1973; Tuckman and Oliver 1968).

Pupil Attitudes to Teacher

A few studies have used pupil ratings of their teachers in order to ascertain how successful a certain treatment has been. The rationale behind this is quite simply that if pupils find their teachers interesting and enjoyable then they are more likely to participate in task-oriented behaviours and less likely to misbehave in class. Thus we should take into account the feelings of pupils in any assessment of teacher competence. Unfortunately studies which attempt to consider this factor are very rare.

The study by Wragg (1971) utilized pupil ratings of student teachers in order to ascertain just how much improvement would take place as a result of microteaching with varying forms of feedback. It was found that the group of students which received both television feedback and feedback from the Flanders Interaction Analysis Category System (FIAC) showed an increased rating of 13 per cent on the reteach, while the groups who received either television feedback alone, FIAC feedback alone or no feedback at all showed no increase in their teach-reteach ratings.

Similarly the study by Fortune et al (1967) used pupils recruited from local high schools in the region of Stanford University. These pupils were trained for a total of six hours in the use of STCAG and were then required to rate the student teachers during their microlessons. These pupil ratings were paired with supervisor ratings and it was found that, as a result of micro-teaching, student teachers increased significantly on nine of the twelve STCAG items. Bush (1966) reporting on the 1963 Stanford Microteaching Clinic found that student teachers who received feedback in the form of pupil ratings improved significantly more in their teaching performance than did those not having access to such feedback, and that these pupil ratings were more reliable than either student or supervisor ratings of the student teachers in microteaching. Once again, microteaching training resulted in significant improvement in the teaching performance of interns as measured by pupil ratings.

Thus it appears that, in those studies which have employed pupil ratings of teacher behaviour, positive results have been found in relation to micro-teaching. One can only hope that in future more researchers will make use of pupil ratings as a measure of teaching performance for use in evaluating the effect of any experimental treatment. The difficulties involved in such a venture are considerable (see Chapter 1) but given time and effort, the problems can be overcome and the results of the few studies which have utilized pupils as raters suggest that it is a very worthwhile exercise.

Trainee Attitudes to their Course of Training
Quite a few researchers have administered some form of feedback question-naire to students who have undergone a course of microteaching in order to ascertain the reactions of these trainees to various elements of their training programme. Gregory (1971) did just this at the University of Rhodesia and found that generally students felt that microteaching had been a useful experience, although certain aspects were viewed more favourably than others. Tutors, for example, were rated poorly while the video playbacks were rated quite highly. Overall, however, Gregory concludes that results tend to suggest a favourable attitude to microteaching because of the practical orientation as opposed to isolated theory. Davis (1970) found that students showed a

favourable attitude to a programme of microteaching which consisted of training in the use of the skill of set induction. Bush (1966) also found that the students in the 1963 Stanford Microteaching Clinic displayed a highly favourable attitude to their training programme. Wright (1973) found that students at Hamilton College of Education became very enthusiastic about microteaching, feeling that there was transfer to classroom teaching and appreciating the structured microteaching situation as opposed to the more open classroom situation. A large number of students were in favour of re-placing part of teaching practice with microteaching, which places the emphasis on coaching rather than on assessment. Similarly Brown (1976) and Perrott et al (1976) both report favourable trainee reactions to microteaching programmes.

Finally, in a piece of research carried out at the Ulster College with pre-service Special Education Teachers, it was found that trainee acceptance of microteaching was at a very high level (Hargie 1977). These students were questioned after completing a programme of microteaching and again after classroom practice and it was found that some 97 per cent felt that micro-teaching had been of use to them in the 'real' situation. In addition only three per cent of students felt that microteaching should be dropped al-together from the training programme, while 93 per cent felt that it should be assessed in some manner. Overall these students felt that microteaching was a useful training programme and that they had benefited from it.

It seems that microteaching is regarded as an effective teacher training tech-nique when the attitude of trainees is used as the criterion. However, most of the studies which use this measure do not report the actual questions asked and replies given, in percentages, and it is therefore difficult to make any firm generalizations with regard to student acceptance of microteaching. At the same time it does appear that where questionnaires have been employed the responses to the questions have been positive in that students seem to value microteaching quite highly.

Increases in Pupil Learning
This is the criterion which has been least used by researchers in order to measure the effectiveness of a microteaching programme. There are some fairly obvious reasons why this is so. Many institutions which employ micro-teaching train students in the use of skills which increase pupil participation, amount and quality of learner initiated questions and decrease teacher talk. It is therefore difficult to assess these skills in terms of measures of pupil learn-ing which take the form of responses to factual items on a test, especially when students are informed that pupils should be taught to think rather than merely memorize factual material. Indeed it seems pointless to train students to encourage critical thinking in pupils and then assess this training in terms

of the pupil's ability to remember facts, since it would appear that the two may not even be correlated. Furthermore many institutions, owing to pressures of time and space, are forced to permit *maximum* microlessons of ten minutes, and it is rather unfair to measure teacher performance in terms of what pupils can remember in such a short time since this would obviously affect the teacher's presentation of the lesson.

It is, we believe, for these reasons that most researchers do not attempt to incorporate measures of pupil learning in their research designs. Perhaps measures of pupil learning may be more effective in relation to teachers of primary school pupils rather than of secondary school pupils. Indeed a study by Wyckoff (1973) would seem to confirm that there is a difference between primary and secondary school children with regard to the relationship between teacher behaviour and pupil learning. Wyckoff carried out an experiment with twelve pre-service teachers selected at random from ninety education students at the University of Massachusetts. In addition forty-eight pupils were recruited from local elementary or secondary schools and ranged in age from nine to seventeen years. The pupils were randomly assigned to teaching stations in groups of four and the twelve teachers were randomly assigned a class of four pupils.

Stimulus variation was the skill utilized in the microlessons, and the use of this skill in teaching a five-minute lesson was compared with the result of teaching the same lesson without using the skill in relation to increases in pupil learning. The results of the experiment are not consistent. Secondary school pupils improved their performance with increases in stimulus variation, whereas elementary school children actually deteriorated on the achievement test with increases in stimulus variation.

Wyckoff hypothesizes that this result may be because stimulus variation distracts younger pupils from attending to the lecture content, whereas it has a positive effect on older pupils. In other words, the relationship between arousal and performance may differ with the age or the IQ of the pupils concerned. Thus it would appear that there is a need for much more age and subject specific research in this area before any definite conclusions can be reached regarding the relationship between teacher performance and pupil learning. This would seem to be a prerequisite of any future attempt to use pupil learning as a measure of successful teaching performance, or as an indicator of which skills should be utilized with various pupils.

Conclusion

It seems that an examination of some of the recent studies which have attempted to assess the success of microteaching, conclusively indicates that a programme of microteaching should be an important element in any teacher training course and that it is a more useful technique than the traditional method of practice teaching. At the same time, it should be noted that a programme of microteaching is intended to complement the teacher training course, and is not intended as a complete replacement for traditional teaching practice. Rather it is a means whereby the trainee can learn to practise those technical skills which will be of value to him in the 'real' situation, and learn to analyse his own teaching behaviour as objectively as possible.

While the actual rationale behind microteaching has proved to be a valid one, it should be pointed out that much research has yet to be carried out in order to refine and improve the effectiveness of this teacher training technique. Many questions remain unanswered, relating to the use of tutors, the length of microlessons, the types of observation schedule to be used in feedback tutorials, the skills to be practised, the number of pupils and the use of 'model' tapes. Having shown that microteaching is effective the way is now open for researchers to concentrate on answering these questions in order that teacher trainees can obtain the maximum possible benefit.

Surveys of Microteaching
A Comparative Account

Prior to our survey in 1975 of microteaching in the United Kingdom, several other examinations of the extent of this technique of training teachers had been made. The first of these was by Blaine E. Ward in the USA, which appeared in 1970. This was followed by Brunner in West Germany (1973), Turney in Australia (1973) and by Falus in the United Kingdom (1975).

Before discussing each of the surveys quoted, we offer some cautionary remarks on this type of research as applied to innovations such as microteaching.

As a descriptive exercise, the survey has several shortcomings, notably that it is a sampling operation that requires inference from the data relating to part of the 'target' population. Statistical inference involves techniques of estimation and testing, and much of survey analysis comes adrift at this stage.

Fortunately for the surveys so far conducted into microteaching, the levels of response have been high enough to satisfy most interested parties. In each case, only a small segment of the respondent population has remained largely unknown in character after the survey. It is possible to infer strongly from the data to the whole area of experience.

One question that should be asked of investigators is: why now? Apart from sheer opportunism in the taking of chances ('no time like the present'), there could be several answers. Some are forthcoming from these studies:

1. Ward argues that needs could be better met if institutions preparing teachers had an awareness of microteaching techniques. His study is based on the Stanford model and he calls on available evidence to show that the need for more effective teaching is met by the microteaching programme. He clearly believes in the benefits and hopes to indicate how these are being dispersed among teacher education curricula in the USA, perhaps to encourage further development.

2. Turney, in noting fairly rapid dissemination of the general idea, drew attention to 'activities which could not be truly called microteaching'. This seems to us a justification of the survey: it can identify and may check any tendency to fill new bottles with old wine, such as describing group practice or closed circuit television recording as microteaching.

3. Our own study was opportune enough: it just preceded drastic reshaping of teacher training in the United Kingdom and came at possibly the peak rate of expansion of microteaching facilities. It also flushed out elements of 'pseudo' microteaching, as did the Australian enquiry, and indicated levels of development, distinguished by Falus in his review. But the reason we prefer to advance is that school practice has shown increasing signs of inadequacy in meeting the requirements of teacher training (Stones and Morris, 1972). We hope to strengthen the claim of microteaching as a complement to, if not a substitute for, practice teaching. Both Turney's and our survey show the location of the one in relation to the other and Turney records opinions on the effectiveness of microteaching against conventional practice. Yet all the surveys take the technique in isolation, though Ward did intend to examine how curricula were adapted in the USA to include microteaching and Falus was to study 'modern methods of teacher training' for UNESCO, with special reference to microteaching, in Sweden, West Germany and the United Kingdom.

Properly, then, the survey method should allow comparison to be made with alternatives to the subject under investigation. A more awkward limitation to the microteaching surveys might be that, whilst the rate of expansion is reasonably well-charted, little light is shed on why this rate is no faster or no slower.

The incentives to adopt microteaching seem clear enough in terms of the drive to raise the standard and the amount of outputs from the teacher training system, and in the given state of technology in education there were no serious technical limitations. So what resistance met the advance of microteaching and why was that resistance so little? The surveys give very few indications of why microteaching was not adopted because the institutions concerned would generally be non-respondents. Exceptionally, our survey noted one or two applications of the technique for corrective purposes only, and Turney found respondents planning use of microteaching for remedial practice in respect of 'particular weaknesses' brought out on school practice. This implies rejection of the behavioural approach to teaching skills, which also emerged as a 'difficulty' in microteaching for some users.

There are, surely, other frictions tending to slow down the progress of microteaching; our point is that the survey method can easily miss such considerations because the researcher may not be looking for them. He may bind his actions by explicit assumptions, an illustration of which is Falus' statement that his data includes most of the colleges and universities using microteaching, an assumption in his view confirmed by the knowledge gained.

A common form of implicit assumption is the framing of questions. Falus admits that answers to one question showed a more advantageous picture than reality would have indicated because it ruled out a possible response. Less obvious than the exclusion of information is the assumption as to who is interested in or who will benefit from the survey or the activity (in this case, mircoteaching). Ward, for instance, looked for observed changes in student attitude toward .education; Turney left open-ended most items of the questionnaire, thus directing his enquiry at the individual experiences of respondents.

A more rigorous kind of assumption is that relating to theoretical knowledge. Two examples here may serve: the design of teaching models for the discrimination of teaching skills and the construction of teaching cycles for improving performance. Ward and Turney examined both these and Brunner in addition the former: he states that trained teaching skills are fields of behaviour rather than operationalized behaviours, implicitly rejecting the over-simplification of teaching performance. The other studies show different theoretical backgrounds in their approach to modelling and their data reflect these backgrounds to some extent; even Falus, who disclaims any clarifying of theoretical issues, finds himself relating a type of modelling to particular research work.

One disappointing feature of the surveys was the lack of propositions that could be tested. We could not claim any distinction for our study, but we did set up some simple hypotheses (see Chapter 4), relating to differences in the nature and development of microteaching facilities. A more serious criticism is that the surveys either did not set clear objectives or did not fulfil those which were set. Turney's work, based on seven points like our own, is least open to such criticism since the objectives were fairly straightforward.

One final comment: survey analysis today can be a highly refined operation, using powerful computer tools. We found no examples of interaction between variables, and much information seems to have been overlooked. Even Ward, who presents her data in the form of tables with groups of respondents and occasionally combines two variables, is not able to draw out a 'typical' facility or offer interesting associations despite the impressive student numbers covered by her survey.

The objective common to all these enquiries was to identify the locations of microteaching activity. This was achieved with considerable, if varying, success judging by the scale and the detail of response. The degree to which microteaching had penetrated institutions of teacher education varied from around 33 per cent in the USA and in West Germany to around 40 per cent in Australia. The level in the United Kingdom could not be determined since Falus' was a selective survey that did not reach all eligible institutions.

The general aim of the studies is less easy to state. Ward (1970) sought understanding of how microteaching is being used. Turney and his colleagues (1973) aimed at an account of practices and problems of microteaching. Falus (1975) saw his study as describing some details of the implementation and application of microteaching, whilst Brunner (1973) set out to 'establish the extent, duration and external organization of microteaching installations' (our translation). It seems fair to describe all four as quantitative surveys, though some definition of microteaching was offered to respondents, certain attitudes to the technique were presented and a little evaluation of existing facilities attempted.

Of the studies, two included research into microteaching as an objective, those by Turney and Falus. Only Ward looked explicitly for modifications on the Stanford programme, but the others all noted the process of differentiation from this model. Turney reported significant variations in implementing the Stanford format by most programmes of microteaching in Australia. Brunner noted a 'distinct trend towards perceptible modification of the original microteaching design' (our translation). Falus asserted a striving to develop methods more suitable for European conditions, but offered no specific supporting evidence. Ward likewise did not provide detailed evidence, though she discerned a general lack of knowledge about the skills of teaching as defined at Stanford.

Although the technical facilities used for microteaching were investigated in all the studies, the approaches taken and the details obtained differed widely. For general purposes the actual number of recording units was the key item. More specific concerns included the type of recording, the use of modelling, the back-up equipment and the flexibility of operation. No study aimed at an economic appraisal of microteaching, though Turney noted the work of Clift et al on its cost effectiveness (1974). Kennedy (1975) has prepared such an analysis for Stirling University, and we attempt (Chapter 8 and Appendix I) a totalling of the cost of equipment and an estimate of the operating costs of facilities.

From these general remarks and illustrations we move now to each of the 'national surveys'.

The USA Survey

It is this survey by Ward (1970) that we shall discuss first of all. Brief accounts have been given elsewhere [(Stones & Morris, 1972); Wragg, (1974); Turney, (1973)], in the context of the function of microteaching in teacher training.

Our examination will be more concerned with appraisal of the survey, not merely of the use of microteaching by American teacher education institutions.

We start by saying bluntly that the enquiry took place too early in the process of development of microteaching. We mean that inevitably less than adequate experience was given by less than satisfactory programmes to large numbers of student teachers. One in four programmes had run for one year only and, with the average lifetime of facilities at the time of survey being just two years, the newness of the technique must have limited the quality of training offered, despite the soundness of the original model.

There are other, more specific ways of revealing limitations of microteaching installations. Ward's survey illustrates several of these:

1. *the proportion of institutions with microteaching*: Ward recorded one in three and this is the lowest of all the surveys;
2. *the number of teacher education courses using microteaching*: in each institution over half of American colleges reported by Ward had only a single course using it. This proportion tends to fall as the duration of microteaching lengthens, but this figure is high.
3. *the frequency of the teach/reteach cycle in microteaching programmes*: this was a standard feature for barely a quarter of Ward's respondents.
4. *the recommended number of teaching encounters in microteaching programmes*: for Ward this number is twenty, and Stones & Morris (1972) infer that a large proportion were not providing adequate experiences for students — it was actually over 99 per cent!
5. *the extent to which videotape recording of microteaching is used*: Ward found, in the analysis of techniques by their relative use, that the largest single group of respondents was that using videotape at least half of the time. However, when numbers were compared with those largely recording by another means or not at all, the videotape users are only three-quarters of the total reported. There remained, it seemed, a sizeable number of institutions not offering this element of the microteaching model to students.
6. *the composition of the microclass*: the Stanford programme used real pupils throughout, not peers of the student teachers. Yet, of those declaring real pupils, only one in five used them at least three-quarters of the time, as against two in three of those declaring peer pupils using them this much.
7. *the frequency of technical skills in the microteaching cycle*: Ward listed the skills of teaching in order of

1. their use by respondents
2. their incidence in teaching models, written or recorded for use by students
3. their rating by importance.

The average ranking of the top five skills (1) fell by one position in terms of the models (2) and by a further two positions in terms of the importance given them (3). This means a displacement by other skills less frequently used at the time of survey but presumably to figure more in future development of microteaching. These skills, ranked by their importance, showed an average improvement of three places compared with their frequency against those used most. The difference in frequency of some four percentage points in the 'teaching only' responses, was doubled for the 'teach/reteach' responses, reflecting in our view the lack of experience in critiques and in modelling of the more exacting skills.

8. *Training of staff in microteaching techniques*: however it stands as an innovation, the 'scaled down teaching encounter' model of practical teaching can only be as productive as the competence of supervisory staff allows. Institutions reporting staff training programmes to Ward displayed considerable awareness and ingenuity of preparation of staff. Programmes ranged from in-service courses, including the induction of new staff, through self-preparation to practical sessions in the teaching units, including demonstrations. The overall impression is sustained by the number of schemes in operation, representing on average one for each institution. Furthermore, in reporting staffing levels for microteaching centres, Ward shows that half of the eight or nine persons typically involved were academic staff. The only possible doubt is the degree of involvement: numbers are not enough, there has to be interest as well. Yet Ward established that most respondents changed their attitude to or behaviour in teaching, for the better in their opinion. It is a little surprising, therefore, to find Ward discerning a need for further study of technical skills alongside her approval of the complete sequence of microteaching used by larger, 'mature' programmes.

A second judgment of the American survey is that its major objectives were not directly served by the mode of inquiry. Ward is much concerned with structural aspects of teacher education curricula, yet she does not present the curricular structure of respondent institutions. The modification of that structure is dealt with solely in terms of course hours, and the respondents divided two to one in favour of inserting microteaching into courses as against adding to the existing length of courses. It is also difficult to detect how the basic Stanford model was modified, since much of Ward's data refer to non-incorporation of that model into curricula: the one in four respondents never using the reteach element of the microteaching cycle; the one in three not recording teaching encounters at least part of the time; the two in three offering fewer than five encounters to students; the one in two using peer pupils not less than three parts of the time; the one in five using at least twice the recommended number of pupils in a microclass. These features can be regarded, not so much as modifications of, as departures from the original.

Finally, we would comment that Ward's enquiry not only failed to answer certain questions but raised others that beg for answers. This she has done by presenting a mass of data, too crudely or too rigidly, which requires speculation or delving by the reader.

The inescapable impression is, for all these criticisms, of the value of Ward's pioneering study. It was clearly well received by those institutions active in microteaching. It had clearly defined terms and models. It asked highly pertinent questions. It gave other researchers both the initiative and a framework to investigate microteaching in other teacher training systems. It provided the greater understanding of microteaching in use that Ward thought was needed and so must surely have helped needs to be better met as she desired.

The Australian Survey

We turn now to the work of Turney and his colleagues in Australia, from which the value of Ward's survey will be much in evidence.

In Australia, says Turney, (1973), the growth of microteaching has been impressively steady, yet it was only introduced some three years prior to his survey. One reason for this advance is the strong influence of the Stanford model, from which most programmes drew their inspiration. The penetration of microteaching was adjudged comparable to that of teacher training courses in the USA, at over half within five years of its initiation. Turney's decision to rule out one in ten of the programmes of 'microteaching' reported was based on inconsistency with the concept, of which signs were provided by the unusually broad range of objectives. Of those quoted as responses (Turney, table 5), only half in our view could be fairly exclusively related to the use of microteaching, and these are concentrated in a handful of objectives, namely:

development of specific teaching skills	25% of items cited
opportunities for specific feedback	11%
provision of 'low-threat' training situation	8%
development of models of teaching behaviour	2%
preparation to face regular practice teaching	4%

We do not regard as specific to microteaching, however worthwhile they may be, such objectives as 'self-analysis of performance', 'awareness', 'confidence', 'critical attitude' or even remedial activity. Each of these can be realised by conventional practice, but Turney shows that his respondents favoured the effectiveness of microteaching. Any weakness of school practice in this respect could well be explained by the characteristic lack of clear objectives or by the mode of assessment. Where microteaching was used as a lead into classroom teaching, as Turney found for at least one in four of programmes, its advantages may have been recognized by staff and by students. The finding that most microteaching took place during school practice is related to the use of children in schools. We do not know if this use was wholly in the microclass receiving a microlesson, but it appears unlikely for some of Turney's respondents.

The effectiveness of microteaching was evaluated in terms of the acquisition, or at least the awareness, of skills. With four or five skills being presented in the average programme, of some thirty hours' duration, awareness seems to us a more likely outcome than acquisition (our survey revealed a ratio of ten hours per skill on average). Moreover, the evaluation took many forms, of which 'discussion' was the most common, being used by half of Turney's respondents and outnumbering the use of schedules of all kinds. A further limitation on effectiveness is the quality of skill being practised: most of the Stanford skills are technical and permit easy recording and appraisal, so they are the most frequently offered to students. To Ward's list of skills most taught and.retaught, Turney adds only the skill of explaining, and from it removes only that of the use of examples. Yet, as Wragg (1974), points out, these skills are 'low inference variables' in behaviour change. The higher order skills, placing more emphasis on the effective aspects of the teacher's role and on the learner's role, contribute importantly to classroom activity, and of these we know very little. Turney's survey, however, does offer 'priority' skills of this nature relating to modelling, which we discuss below.

The analysis of skills is one way of assessing how effective microteaching is, but it is limited in several respects. In particular, isolating component skills in a controlled situation 'disintegrates' the teaching process so that students can 'master' the model. Apart from the requirement to put the skills together, microteaching has itself to be 'integrated' with other elements in teacher training courses, or else operate as a unit in its own right. Turney found no formal linking with other units for one respondent in four, others having varying degrees of integration, most commonly with practice teaching but also with curriculum studies.

The microteaching cycle can be considered as a determinant of effectiveness. As such it could include the prior assessment of teaching competence. The Australian pattern displayed little pre-experience evaluation and followed the cycle presented by the researchers: viewing a model, teaching, receiving feedback, reteaching. Only this last stage was never used by the majority of respondents. This compares unfavourably with American and British experience of three in four institutions using the reteach. Its explanation, suggests Turney, lies in the pressure on resources (usually staff!).

Another source of pressure in microteaching programmes is the micro-lesson; where it is taught, and to whom. Remarkably, half the Australian institutions used both college and school locations, though concentrating the use of units on-site and of real pupils in these locations. All programmes considered, three in four used real pupils — twice the frequency in the USA and higher than that in the United Kingdom. Yet the problem of access to such pupils remained acute for some programmes.

Possibly the strongest feature of Turney's survey is the data on modelling. As an important step to microteaching practice, teacher education programmes are increasingly using modelling. Respondents were unanimous on the need for high-quality models and the order of preference of skills differed from that of use, as in Ward's study, if only slightly. Of twelve skills listed by use and by priority, six technical skills topped the first list, their average ranking six places higher than that of six skills centering about the individual child. In the second list, this ranking was only three places higher as 'discipline' and 'small group teaching' especially displaced the technical skills in some measure. Curiously, this improvement coincided with that estimated from similar data in Ward's report (see above, p 33), and Turney discerned a trend away from teacher-oriented skills. This may be so, but the materials widely used to supplement both real and model teaching performance were still highly specific to analysis of skills.

This analysis occurred during replay sessions as an aid to acquisition of skills of students. It was conducted by supervisory staff, by the student or his peers, and by real pupils in a ratio of 10:5:1. Ward had in contrast reported much more involvement of pupils in the critique stage, twice as often as not. What she did not find was much evidence of self-evaluation by students, which featured in one-third of Australian microteaching programmes. The propor-tion of these using written rationale for skills, at one in five, was matched in only four of the Stanford skills by American programmes. These came out even less favourably in comparison of media for modelling: videotaping was so used by fewer than 10 per cent, against the 37 per cent quoted by Turney for Australian programmes.

The really distinctive and, in our view, the outstanding aspect of the Australian survey was its emphasis on the difficulties presented by micro-teaching facilities. These included both familiar problems of resource alloca-tion and less obvious ones of attitudes and demands. Excluded, perhaps sur-prisingly, were drawbacks associated with some theoretical underpinnings of microteaching practice and with the assessment of teaching performance. This last had long been a difficulty with conventional teaching practice, and indeed there are few problems that it does not share with microteaching in some respect. This assertion may need support, and it is forthcoming from Turney's summary.

Firstly, there is the sheer volume of student demand. Since school practice is obligatory in most teacher education systems, and microteaching is not, the problem differs as to scale. Yet, for particular institutions, it can be more acute for microteaching. Turney reports large numbers of students scheduled for programmes, and this is only one of the logistic requirements, but school practice must always have been a major headache for administrators. The 'scaling down' of microteaching offers an inbuilt safety valve for programmes under stress that is scarcely available for 'real' teaching. We do not know student numbers in microteaching in Australia from this survey but one in three respondents were planning in terms of 100 or more in 1973, similar to Ward's data for 1969.

A discussion of microteaching and teaching practice

The matter of scheduling, not apparently difficult for American institutions, was an embarrassment for several Australian ones with the existence of over-loaded courses into which proper integration was hardly possible. This situation occurs for school practice, because of its length, its distribution through courses, its location and its shortcomings as a method. Microteaching has been fitted, if not integrated, into courses, as experience shows, even at the cost of excluding some of its features. This paring down of programmes is not without support among the innovators, making a virtue of necessity.

Staffing of microteaching units is partly a question of providing sufficient numbers trained to operate or maintain them (Turney notes that half his respondents encountered problems in one or the other). It is also a question of attitude: many Australian programmes were still dependent on perhaps a single initiator, lacking support from colleagues with the same interest (and we gained this impression from our own survey, Chapter 6 below). Recent developments in self-analysis by students, of which there was evidence in Turney's study, offer prospect of relief of the staffing problem in that staff can withdraw from a tutorial to a supervisory role (Brown, 1975). Progress in this direction for school practice, thus easing a still greater pressure on staff, is likely to follow but at a slower pace, given the difficulties of (a) structuring the teaching situation with appropriate 'dimensions' of skills, and of (b) appraisal of performance in selected situations.

Self-analysis would require student attitudes favouring the teaching experience, and here we find traditional methods of practice consistently emerging from research studies with highly favourable responses. Yet microteaching is establishing itself with students: they were found by Turney to be assessing their own performance on one in three programmes, by us to be doing so in groups more than singly, for a quarter of the respondents, and by

Ward to show 'concern' for self-evaluation, by one in every five.

An important influence on students' attitudes could be their awareness of how practical teaching experience fits into the training curriculum as preparation for their role as employed teachers. What Edith Cope (1970) euphemistically calls an 'integrated system' is at least as well served by microteaching as by school practice, and she shows convincingly that a large minority of student teachers responding to her survey reported little or no benefit from supervision by college or school staff. Contact with fellow-students, though not in the form of evaluation, was consistently rated more highly.

We conclude from analysis of Cope's findings that students contributed most, in their view, to their learning during periods of school experience in training.

If this finding were valid for the microteaching experience, this would strongly suggest its being favourably regarded by students. Turney (1973) found that peers were analysing teaching performance on one programme in four, and Ward reported three respondents in five quoting 'pupils' as involved in the critique stage, a ratio corresponding closely to those largely relying on peers for the microclass.

We are saying, in effect: students, if they are to be assessed, prefer to be assessed by their fellows, and most of all by themselves. Microteaching performance, permitting self-evaluation, would register highly with students. Since microteaching is moving away from supervision, we would not regard student attitudes as a problem in its development.

The attitudes of real pupils were not sampled in any way by Turney or by Ward, but evidence suggests (Cope 1970) that school practice, albeit with 'captive' pupils, was valued highly in respect of relationships built up with pupils by student teachers. Objectives classified as affective would be served well by school practice in many instances. The microteaching programme is not well suited, in its form of a cycle involving rotation of the microclass, to developing relationships, and the skills on which it most relies are not of the higher order variety.

Clearly, the Australian experience raised some fascinating possibilities and associated difficulties for microteaching. It showed that much better quality information and materials, requiring further research, are needed if its 'great promise' is to be fulfilled. Turney concluded, not surprisingly, that this promise depends on the fact that microteaching was fast becoming an established teacher education procedure, an impression we see no reason to challenge on the data he provided.

The West German Survey

The survey by Brunner carried out in 1972 among colleges of teacher education in West Germany was limited in scope. Its timing, six years after the launching of microteaching at Tübingen University, seemed appropriate. It did not include all potential users and received a modest enough response of some thirty institutions using the technique.

In relative terms, as noted above, Brunner's rate of response was comparable to that for other surveys, but student numbers reported on microteaching programmes were disappointing, averaging about forty-five. Moreover, Brunner concluded that the discrepancy between practice and the form of organization considered appropriate [the model] was a sign of inexpertness of treatment by colleges.

He cited, as evidence for his claim that the original system was applied fairly freely, the frequency with which a microclass was used that was much larger (more than ten pupils) than for the Stanford model. The proportion of large to small classes varied according to the use of real or peer pupils: for peers, the ratio was only 1:8, for peers and real pupils as alternatives, 1:4 and for real pupils alone, 1:1. In effect, in schools microteaching was conducted with a macroclass as often as not.

Further indication of how the original model was modified in German programmes was given in terms of the control of variables in the microteaching situation. Three in four respondents reported increasingly complex training, in respect particularly of pupil numbers and teaching skills, compared with standard microteaching procedure. The range of skills offered in more than one programme was restricted in number and type, the only surprising feature being the leading preference: discussion methods. Brunner found general agreement on the benefits of microteaching and also on the need to develop more reliable instruments of observation and analysis, and Turney (1973) was to confirm this finding for Australian programmes in his survey.

The United Kingdom Survey

The last survey we shall discuss is that by Falus of the United Kingdom in 1974. This pre-dated our own by a year only, and yet the differences are considerable in the objectives set, the data obtained and in some interpretations offered.

Falus' main objective was a comprehensive picture, but he limited his questioning to encourage respondents. Certainly they responded well, and permitted him to estimate at least thirty-five to forty institutions using microteaching. His data were organized in two ways: according to the sequence of questions, for which many modifications were suggested but from which frequencies could be drawn up; and according to the consensus of responses or typical solutions.

The survey's most successful inquiry was on the component skills of the microteaching programmes, regarded as the leading objective. Although the emphasis once again was heavily on the technical, teacher-oriented skills, the average number presented was three. Systematic observation was widely reported with respect to the feedback stage, but an element in programmes that Turney (1973) found significant — that of modelling — was poorly developed.

The microclass was presented generally along the lines of the Stanford model by half the respondents, but very few were found to satisfy all requirements of microteaching in its strict sense. The reasons for this disappointing finding (with which we substantially agree) were conceived by Falus largely in terms of material provision, such as of equipment and of the supply of real pupils.

One feature of the 1974 survey not contained in any other is its reference to inservice teacher education. One in five institutions claimed to operate microteaching in this area. However, we found three-quarters of our 1975 respondents active in microteaching officially stating that they offered inservice courses to teachers (ATCDE, 1976). Allen and Ryan (1969) had already designated such courses as the most suited to development of microteaching, so Falus' impressions may not have borne close relation to the facts or may have revealed a state of neglect.

Some Conclusions from the Surveys
What are the overall impressions that we gain from this series of surveys of microteaching? There are so many points of view as to what constitutes a successful study that we would not receive general agreement by saying that, together or separately, the surveys made a valuable contribution to the knowledge of teacher education methods. This may be true of one and not others, and we would be justifying our own exercise in the field. At the least, it is fair to claim as much value as for other surveys, such as of the bibliographies of microteaching. The reader, however, deserves always to know if his efforts are worth the making. For him we offer just a few comments on these investigations.

Firstly, they all give the impression of an innovation soundly conceived but less soundly implemented. The shortfalls from the original microteaching models may correspond to shortcomings. Yet there were many examples of 'mature' programmes in operation and of supportive research projects aimed at improving effectiveness in operation.

Secondly, there was no indication of any falling away in the use of the technique, though the rate at which programmes were being set up was not examined in any study (except our own, Chapter 5 below). We shall examine, in the final chapter on the future of microteaching, whether there are signs of departure from the method.

Thirdly, the studies do not provide evidence of nation-wide, let alone world-wide, acceptance and use of microteaching. There are major teacher education systems still to be surveyed or still to show signs of implementing the innovation, despite the interest in developments shown by international organisations such as OECD (1975) and UNESCO (1974).

Again, no survey seems to have combined satisfactorily both breadth and depth of investigation, particularly in respect of the contribution to the quality of teacher education programmes. The way seems clear to attempt further penetration into some of these, such as of inservice training and of higher education institutions.

Further research may indeed be worthwhile and forthcoming, to which we ourselves hope to contribute. The clear impression we have of the research discussed in this chapter is of its origin in the discipline of psychology. All the authors had such a theoretical background, and this cast reflections on their patterns of inquiry.

Apart from the stress on behavioural aspects of teaching displayed by the surveys, the influence of psychology was evident from the interest in modelling, directed as it seemed largely at the teacher, and (to a lesser extent) in attitudes, whether of teaching staff or of students.

The final impression, left till last since we think it the most significant, is that the surveys of microteaching tapped an eagerness to exploit the innovation and to communicate experience of it. What this tells us about the personnel responding to the inquiries is open to endless speculation. We offer just one conjecture: that for too long too many teachers, including their trainers, have regarded teaching as subjective experience, unsuitable for analysis because it is personal and complex. It is sometimes necessary to simplify experience, and we concluded that willingness to entertain doing this was shown by the proponents of microteaching.

Sometimes, however, it is also necessary to complicate things, and what the surveys should have impressed on us, perhaps, is that the breakdown of the teaching situation can go too far. Far enough, in effect, means just to preserve relationships between pupils and teacher and between the pupils themselves. Are we now witnessing that necessary, if not scientific, complication in training that best prepares students for the art of teaching? This question of the appropriate dimensions of teaching we shall attempt to answer in Chapter 7 and as part of our conclusion on the prospects for microteaching.

Microteaching in the British Isles
Part I of the Survey

By 1975, the end of the first decade of microteaching in the United Kingdom
was approaching. It seemed appropriate to conduct an inquiry into its development. A number of objectives of such an inquiry presented themselves, as
outlined below. Of especial interest to us was to what extent microteaching
activities had modified the original Stanford model. For this reason we did
not attempt any definition of microteaching. What we did try was the framing of questions that would permit a variety of microteaching activities to be
presented by respondents.' From this variety we hoped to abstract a 'typical'
facility. This would have as many as possible of the most common features,
expressed as responses to questions.

This 'modal' model of microteaching would display a number of features
that did not appear in the Stanford model, and would lack a few that did.
Arguably, we could maintain that the diversified practices of microteaching in
Britain represented improvement on the original. However, American practice
had already diversified as Ward's (1970) survey showed.

The scale of the survey is claimed as national, as no group of teacher
training establishments (outside the defence service) was excluded, and response from every group was received at both stages of the survey. The number
of establishments drawn from the source was 243 (ATCDE, 1975), and this
was increased by eight mainly by bringing in polytechnics newly involved in
teacher training. However, the original population of colleges and departments was reduced by several factors. One of these factors was the lack of any
direct involvement in teacher training. This largely was reported by university
departments of eudcation but also by establishments training in the arts,
offering main subject tuition to students who enrolled elsewhere for teacher
training. There were also, during 1975, decisions taken to suspend initial
training at several colleges, and very few of these could respond positively to

the survey.

We settled the final total of the 'target' population at 220 (Appendix I), but among the non-respondents there may have been more not organised for the training of teachers. The population was separated into four groups by financial status: local authority, voluntary, university and polytechnic. The overall response rate to Part I, with 177 replies, was 80 per cent and this was achieved entirely by postal communication. One element in the survey procedure which proved effective was the despatch of 'follow-up' letters, each of which increased the response to Part I by a good margin.

The introductory questionnaire, Part I, was designed to achieve the objective of identifying areas of microteaching among colleges and departments of education and research being carried on. It included questions on staff and students, numbers and courses provided and planned. We added the variables of financial status and distance from London, and table 4.1 shows the distribution of the 220 'target' establishments and of the respondents by status.

4.1 *Financial status of teacher training establishments*

Part I		Local authority	Voluntary	University	Polytechnic	Total*
Recipients	No	110	54	42	14	220
	%	50	25	19	6	100
Respondents	No	88	37		12	177
	%	50	23	21	7	100 +
Respondents % Recipients		80	74	88	86	80

* includes 'proxy' responses
+ total does not equal 100 due to rounding

The largest group of local authority colleges included in Scotland those colleges centrally financed by government. Of those establishments not responding to Part I of the questionnaire, no one financial status took a disproportionate share of the total non-responses. Similarly, there were no great differences in the proportions of each status group responding to Part I and in the proportions declaring and detailing microteaching activity, whether planned or operational (table 4.2).

4.2 *Respondents to Part I and microteaching activity*

Response	Colleges	Departments	Total
	%	%	%
A To part I	78	88	80
B Microteaching activity as of			
Part I	79	75	78

A difference that made analysis of the preliminary responses more involved was that of geographical location. This showed a distinctive 'centrifugal' tendency (table 4.3).

4.3 *Microteaching activity and distance from London*

Microteaching	Mean distance	Standard deviation
	Kilometres	
A Active N = 113	176	130
B Prospective N = 25	147	127
C Inactive N = 39	129	87

The differences in distance from London are statistically significant for 'active' respondents against others (to the 0.1% level of confidence) and for 'prospective' against 'inactive' respondents (to the 5.0% level). Location of activity in Scotland and Northern Ireland heavily weights the mean distance for Group A, as does the infrequent location of activity in London for Group C.

We can now look at the responses to Part I of the questionnaire and its parameters of staff and students, courses and microteaching activity. This last will be related to the others singly and in combination. It will be analysed in three ways:

  a. by single category of establishment, whether 'active', 'prospective' or 'inactive' in microteaching;
  b. by distinction between 'active' and other establishments;
  c. by distinction between 'inactive' and other establishments.

This means that respondents planning microteaching ('prospective') will be associated with each of the other categories for particular purposes.

Staff in teacher training establishments
We present firstly the distribution of staff by sex over the three levels of microteaching activity (table 4.4). To aid comparison we add the distinction between two groups of activity.

4.4 *Staff numbers in teacher training institutions*

Microteaching	Sample size (N)	Male staff average	Female staff number	All staff number
Active (A)	99	44	18	62
Prospective (B)	21	41	28	69
Inactive (C)	25		19	52
A + B	120	44	20	63
C	25	33	19	52
A	99	44	18	62
B + C	46	37	23	60

The most obvious fact about returns of staff numbers is that they were larger for respondents active and prospective in microteaching. Yet the difference as against inactive respondents of eleven staff is entirely explained by male members and it is significant to the 0.1% level of confidence.

The ratio of male to female staff varied by microteaching status. It averaged 68%:32% overall, but reached 71 per cent male staff for respondents active in microteaching compared with only 62 per cent for those prospective or inactive. The overall difference is significant to the 5 per cent level, but for active respondents again to the 0.1% level, due largely in our view to the staffing ratios in university departments.

Students in Training
The average enrolment of respondent teacher training establishments, at 570, showed interesting variations. Since teacher-student ratios are regulated, no variations were expected or recorded as against microteaching activity. The same pattern of significantly larger numbers (by 27%) for active or prospective respondents than for those inactive comes out clearly (table 4.5).

4.5 *Student numbers in teacher training institutions*

Microteaching	Number	Male students	Female students	All students
			average number	
Active (A)	99	196	404	600
Prospective (B)	21	163	470	633
Inactive (C)	25	117	359	476
A + B	120	191	416	606
C	25	117	359	476
A	99	196	404	600
B + C	46	138	408	546

The sex-ratios are neatly reversed compared with staff numbers, with 70 per cent female students as against 30 per cent female staff. The same variation with microteaching activity is observed: male students are 33 per cent of the total for 'active' respondents, compared with the 25 per cent for others. An encouraging sign is the large number of female students likely to gain access to microteaching facilities, reflected in the female staff numbers reported by prospective respondents.

To summarise the differences in staffing and enrolments, ratios of one to the other are presented in table 4.6.

4.6 *Staffing and student numbers*

Microteaching	Number of Units	Male students Male staff	Female students Female staff	All students All staff
Active (A)	99	4.5	22.4	9.7
Prospective (B)	21	4.0	16.8	9.1
Inactive (C)	25	3.5	18.9	9.2

The data show that a higher concentration of male students to male staff occurs in microteaching establishments than in others. This raises the question of whether there could be a differentiation of quality in training of teachers associated with male dominance! The discussion in Chapter 2 of the effectiveness of microteaching should suggest the answer that male students are more likely to be offered more effective training.

The provision of courses

We analysed the returns for existing courses, testing the idea that micro-teaching was more likely with higher levels of course provision. Active respondents did report slightly higher proportions of degree courses to the total but no more courses than other respondents. The average number of five courses overall was distributed between degree and non-degree courses in the ratio of 1:2.

Plans for microteaching were not associated with plans for courses any more than activity was linked with currently operating courses. Roughly half of all respondents to Part I declared the number of new courses, and these were distributed by microteaching status much as for the response in general.

This was the case even when we isolated respondents planning new courses at only one level, degree or non-degree. Those active in microteaching reported five more staff on average, with a 5 per cent higher proportion of males at 70 per cent, than other respondents planning courses at both levels (table 4.7).

4.7 *Staff numbers and new courses*

Type of course	Active in microteaching				Prospective or inactive in microteaching			
	Male staff		Female staff		Male staff		Female staff	
	AvNo	%	AvNo	%	AvNo	%	AvNo	%
Degree only N = 31	45	70	19	30	37	63	22	37
Non-degree only N = 12	50	70	21	30	43	68	20	32
Average	46	70	20	30	40	65	21	35

The difference between average numbers of staff for the two categories of microteaching is entirely accounted for by male staff.

If local authority colleges were isolated, the association of staff numbers with microteaching activity would be accentuated (table 4.8).

4.8 *New courses and staff numbers in local authority colleges*

Microteaching activity	Degree courses only			Non-degree courses only		
	Male	Female	Total	Male	Female	Total
	AvNo %	AvNo %	AvNo	AvNo %	AvNo %	AvNo
A (N = 13)	82 71	34 29	116	63 68	29 32	92
B + C (N = 5)	13 45	15 55	29	38 60	29 40	63

To summarize, the larger colleges with higher proportions of male staff plan higher level courses.

If the differences with respect to new courses are not spectacular, it is possible at least to show the continuum from degree course/microteaching activity to non-degree course/microteaching inactivity (table 4.9).

4.9 *Planning of courses and microteaching activity*

Provision \ Status	Active respondents	Prospective respondents	Inactive respondents	All
	%	%	%	%
Degree courses N = 31	81	10	10	100*
Degree and non-degree courses N = 23	70	22	9	100*
Non-degree courses N = 12	58	25	17	100*
Total N = 66	73	17	11	100*

*Percentages do not total due to rounding

The distinction between degree and non-degree courses is a crude one. Since we did not intend to examine curricula of training establishments, we spared respondents the trouble of specifying higher degrees, short courses and in-service provision for teachers. The information obtained did allow us to distinguish between respondents at each of the three levels of microteaching activity as in tables 4.8 and 4.9. We conclude firmly that the relationship of staff numbers to the planning of courses depended on the level of those courses, if not on the number, and on the level of microteaching activity.

Conclusion

This preliminary analysis of the survey data has been largely a matter of tracing certain features of the responding institutions, estimating the scale of involvement in microteaching and relating those features to that involvement. Care is essential in exploring data for the purpose of stressing any contribution by a single variable. Selvin and Stuart (1966) warn against 'data dredging', Moser and Kalton (1971) against 'attempting to test an hypothesis on the same data that generated it'.

The timing of the survey was in our view amply justified. There had been surveys of the literature, samples of microteaching activity, several conferences and still no comprehensive inquiry into the practice of microteaching in Britain. Such an inquiry seemed overdue (it had been carried out in other countries, as noted in Chapter 3) but ours proved timely because it just preceded the most far-reaching and long-term changes in the system for training teachers in its long history. The survey can serve as a point of reference for future appraisals or microteaching, after the outright closures, the amalgamation and redesignation of many colleges and their integration into polytechnic departments of education.

We based the survey on the use of computer analysis of mail questionnaires and on a framework of objectives. These objectives were partly of identification and partly of estimation. We aimed to identify in Part I the locations of microteaching operations and plans, and whether research was proceeding, the methods of operation of microteaching. We hoped to estimate the scale of staffing resources and of the provision of courses, as well as student numbers as a guide to the output from microteaching capacity.

Data existed which provided a background for the analysis of responses to Part I of the survey and carried serious implications for the future development of teacher training and thereby for microteaching:

1. estimates were recorded of the current level of student enrolments, (Association of Teachers in Colleges and Departments of Education, 1976).
2. quotas were agreed or laid down for student enrolments in the circulars of the Department of Education and Science.
3. statistical projections were made of the number of teachers required in the 1980s (DES 1975).

We thought that larger establishments directly financed from public funds would be more likely to develop microteaching facilities. Regional variations were anticipated, possibly related to centres of microteaching activity and research established in the mid-1960s, notably in Scotland and Northern Ireland.

An early overall impression we gained was of the difference in response by location at various points of reference in the survey: membership of the 'target' population, response to Part I, declaration of microteaching activity, response to Part II of the questionnaire. The wastage of response between the two parts clearly lessened the greater the distance from London (see table 5.2 below).

Of the substantial proportion of teacher training establishments yet to develop or to plan microteaching in 1975, most were in the south of England, as implied by tables 4.3 and 5.2 (below). One possible reason is the lack of initiative at the university institute level; university departments of education also did not appear solidly behind the development of microteaching, and they were the only group to declare no planning of this activity.

One might expect institutions that combine teaching with research to offer leadership in educational innovation. It would appear that individual researchers or tutors brought about this particular change as part of their function in universities. We indicate in Chapter 5 the length of experience in microteaching (tables 5.3 and 5.4) and in Chapter 6 those universities quoted as sources of microteaching by respondents to Part II or III of the questionnaire.

Throughout the survey, such impressions as of male dominance of microteaching are qualified by the variation between respondents. The sex ratio of staff varied according to the provision of new courses, to the financial status of respondents, to the level of microteaching activity.

It is time now to take the examination of microteaching a stage further and provide a foundation of fact and interpretation on which we can build a conception of microteaching that will reach the exacting requirements of effective teaching over at least the next decade.

Microteaching in the British Isles
Part II of the Survey

The more detailed investigation of existing or planned microteaching facilities was related to a number of objectives. These were to identify research, to estimate student demand and the scale of provision for microteaching, and to identify methods of operation. Some prediction of microteaching capacity was hoped for and, most speculatively of all, an evaluation was projected of the techniques surveyed as against the traditional model of school experience or 'teaching practice' and against the body of research summarized in Chapter 1. We approached this evaluation of microteaching in terms of alternative 'models' built into Part II of the questionnaire (see fig. 5.3 below, p. 53).

The 'target' population for this part of the survey was identified from responses to Part I that stated activity in or plans for microteaching practice in some form, and the response to Part II was 60 per cent of these. We found the data sufficient for simple analysis, including the relation to variables recorded in Part I.

Part II of the questionnaire was designed for those operating microteaching facilities and Part III for those planning them. Forty per cent of the target population of 220 completed Part II or III and respondents answered a very high proportion of the questions. Only six of the questionnaires recorded had too few responses to be included in the analysis, and one institution provided three questionnaires, which we recorded separately because of its large enrolment.

The analysis of the eighty-four questionnaires considered sufficiently detailed was conducted largely by computer with respect to the structured or numerical responses. What we call 'text' responses required manual collation.

The distinction between active and prospective microteaching will be relaxed for Part II respondents. Only one in eight of the satisfactory returns was by a 'prospective' respondent, on Part III of the questionnaire.

Among the respondents to Part II or III there was very little variation by financial status, but it favoured the colleges and not the departments of education (table 5.1).

5.1 *Respondents to Part II by financial status*

Status and response	Local authority	Voluntary	University	Polytechnic	Total
	%	%	%	%	%
Part II of Part III	N = 46	N = 22	N = 15	N = 5	N = 88
% of Part I recipients	42	41	36	36	40
% of Parts II and III recipients	— — — — 61 — — —		— — — — — 54 — — — —		— — —

There was much more variation in response by area, and table 5.2 reinforces the impression of 'centrifugal' location of genuine microteaching installations given by responses to Part I (table 4.3).

5.2 *Respondents to Part II by area*

Area ╲ Response	London	Rest of England and Wales	S & NI	Total
Part II	6	70	12	88
Of Part I recipients	19%	38%	57%	40%

This suggests the importance of regional centres of microteaching, and in Northern England, in Scotland and Northern Ireland they figure most prominently.

We anticipated that our survey would disclose a modest number of microteaching installations of generally recent date. We were pleasurably surprised by numbers approaching three figures. It was no less a revelation to find the average lifetime as long as three years by the session of 1975-6. Any interpretation of this fact had to take into account variations, by region and by financial status and in the rate of increase over time, which an average would mask.

We present (in table 5.3) the pattern of experience in microteaching. showing the variations by region and by status.

5.3 Years' experience in microteaching, 1966-75

Area \ Status	Average numbers of years			
	Local authority status	Voluntary status	University/ Polytechnic status	Average
England & Wales	N = 34 3.2	N = 2.1	N = 17 3.8	3.0
Scotland, Northern Ireland	N = 10 2.7	N = 2 0.5	N = 3 6.7	3.2
Average	3.1	1.9	4.2	3.1

There was no difference in the lifetimes of microteaching installations by area. Variations emerged only when respondents were additionally classified by status. Departments of education had had microteaching for a year longer than local authority colleges, and these for a year longer than voluntary colleges.

Analysed in terms of a 'moving' average over five years, the trend was for the mean duration of facilities to rise more steeply for departments than for colleges. For all respondents, a slower rate of expansion is predicted, as shown by an overall increase in the 1970s in the average lifetime of microteaching units (table 5.4).

From the trend we estimated a yearly rise in the number of installations. At five per year this would bring the total to 100 by 1978, excluding closures of colleges and microteaching units. This expansion would come from the colleges, a dozen of which stated plans for microteaching without giving details for Part II, and not from the departments.

*5.4 Years' experience: five-year moving averages**

Period Status	1966-70	1967-71	1968-72	1969-73	1970-74	1971-75
Colleges	1.20	1.06	1.24	1.62	1.61	1.63
Departments	2.14	1.20	1.09	1.92	2.14	2.62
Averages	1.50	1.11	1.19	1.70	1.73	1.84

*These apply to the middle year of five years in successive periods with the effect of 'smoothing out' variations into a trend.

In broad terms, a constant value for years' experience, as for colleges in the last three periods, indicates a unitary rate of expansion, and a rising value a slowing down of that rate. It seems clear from the data that departments have had their expansion; returns to Part I show very few with plans for microteaching, and none of these for a university department.

The proportion of establishments with microteaching capacity for a year or less in 1975 was greater for England and Wales than for Scotland and Northern Ireland (table 5.5) showing the later entry of the former establishments into microteaching activity. Much of the difference was accounted for by colleges of education, with a proportion of recent capacity of 44%.

5.5 Proportion of respondents with fewer than two years' microteaching experience

Area Status	England & Wales	Scotland & N Ireland	Average %
Local authority	N = 34 % 38	N = 10 % 10	N = 44 % 32
Voluntary	N = 18 57	N = 2 100	N = 20 60
University/ Polytechnic	N = 17 24	N = 3 0	N = 20 20
Average %	39 N = 69	20 N = 15	36 N = 84

Departments of education in England and Wales had had microteaching for an average of four years, a year longer than colleges. For Scotland and Northern Ireland the difference was four years, in favour of departments of education.

Since the duration of microteaching relates to the number of courses using it, departments had more courses with microteaching than colleges (on average one more course for every two establishments). In England and Wales more establishments had fewer than two courses with microteaching elements than in Scotland and Northern Ireland, 41% compared with 33% (table 5.6). However, this difference is entirely due to colleges of education, for which the proportion is 45%.

5.6 Proportion of respondents with microteaching on a single course

Status＼Area	England & Wales	Scotland & N Ireland	Average %
Local authority	N = 32 50	N = 10 30	N = 42 45
Voluntary	N = 17 35 50	N = 2	N = 19 35
University/ Polytechnic	N = 6 31	N = 3 33	N = 19 31
Average %	N = 65 41	N = 15 33	N = 80* 40

* 4 respondents quoted no course with microteaching

To illustrate even more finely, let us compare the colleges of 'voluntary' status with departments in universities and polytechnics. Sixty per cent (60%) of the latter had microteaching before 1972, against only twenty per cent of the colleges of religious foundation, which have come late into the use of this facility but whose involvement now matches that of the departments. This is so at least in proportion to their total number, and quite arguably in terms of development of the basic model of microteaching. For example, of the seven establishments in the United Kingdom that reported having all the most typical features of microteaching, five were of voluntary status.

Once we introduce the number of courses containing an element of micro-teaching, (table 5.7) we can relate years' experience to curriculum develop-ment. The number of courses could hardly be expected to match the increase in years' experience, but they did so with voluntary colleges. The disparity was greatest for university departments, which was consistent with the slowing rate of expansion of microteaching.

5.7 Microteaching experience and course development

Status	Years' experience Average No	Courses with microteaching Average No
Local authority colleges	3.1	2.4
Voluntary colleges	1.9	2.1
Departments	4.2	2.9

For the longest established capacity of eight to nine years, the ratio was three years for every course, showing the inevitable slowing of the extension of microteaching to courses., However, more of the courses proposed by teacher training establishments were at degree level and such courses make more use of microteaching, as we have indicated above (table 4.9). We did not request information on in-service courses for teachers which would justify separate inquiry, as undertaken by Strasdowsky (1976).

One of the most difficult of our detailed enquiries, for respondents to the survey, concerned the location of periods of teaching practice in the curricula of teacher training courses. We expected students to participate in micro-teaching before their placements for school experience. We anticipated some follow-up activity, including provision for remedial microteaching. We allowed for microteaching during teaching practice, but expected little res-ponse. One response we did not expect was that microteaching replaced teaching practice, as on courses designed for overseas students (University of Leeds).

Not all respondents could meet the request to state the usual location of teaching practice. On one-year courses (frequently regarded as the fourth year of an existing course) there were often two periods, and multiple responses matched the number of the most frequent single location. We scored these responses separately but they can be combined, as can the fourth year with first year locations (table 5.8).

5.8 Location of microteaching in courses

Year of course	Single locations				Multiple locations		
	A	B	C	Total	A	B	C
1st or 4th	33	0	5	38	19	4	14
2nd	10	0	2	12	3	3	3
3rd	2	0	0	2	3	0	1
Total	45	0	7	52	25	7	18

A = before teaching practice (60% of total)
B = during teaching practice
C = after teaching practice (24% of total)

Of the three elements in staff preparation, rating of teaching practice, wherever located in respect to microteaching, showed consistent returns. For the other elements a clear difference emerged (table 5.9).

5.9 Teaching practice and staff preparation for microteaching

Item	Location of microteaching			
	Pre experience +		Post experience	
	No of responses	%	No of responses	%
Training in skills	24	41	8	33
Discussion in seminars	35	59	16	67
Both	59*	100	24*	100

+ 1st or 2nd year of course   * These are not respondent totals

The Scale of Microteaching

We come now to one of the most intriguing aspects of the survey: the scale of microteaching operations. We can make fairly reliable estimates of student numbers and of operating time in microteaching units. Numbers can be related to total enrolments in teacher training, to revised quotas and to respondents' enrolments. Contact hours can be associated with student numbers and projections attempted, but responses here were less satisfactory and data should be treated with reservation.

5.10 Student numbers in microteaching units

Status \ Students	Average numbers			
	1974-5		1975-6	
	Male	Female	Male	Female
Local authority	56	58	68	73
Voluntary	35	50	47	48
University/Polytechnic	36	45	47	48
	N = 66		N = 50	
Total	46	53	52	57
% increase	-	-	13	8

It is apparent, and we use the word with caution, that financial status does influence the involvement of students in microteaching. This is especially true of the rate of increase, between 1974-5 and 1975-6, which disguises marked contrast between types of establishment: increases of 24% and 12% respectively for local authority colleges and for universities and polytechnics, and a contraction of 14% in student involvement amongst voluntary colleges. A second disparity seemed likely between the sexes; male students were expected to rise in number during 1975-6 by 13%, and female students by only 8%. The extremes here were remarkable. Male students in microteaching in universities and polytechnics were to increase by a third during 1975-6.

In order to offer a prediction of student numbers, we used a simple 'moving average' of the estimates for 1974-5 to 1976-7 thus providing an estimate of numbers for 1975 and 1976 as the 'mid-points' (table 5.11).

5.11 Trends in student numbers in microteaching, 1974-77

Numbers \ Years	1974-75/1975-76	1975-76/1976-77
Male students	49	52
Female students	55	59
Total students	104	111

We have already shown that staff numbers are related to microteaching activity (table 4.4). This relationship can be further illustrated by student involvement (table 5.12).

5.12 Student numbers in microteaching and male staff in training establishments

Year Male staff	1974-5		1975-6	
	Male students	Female students	Male students	Female students
	average numbers		average numbers	
1-24	N = 17 26	34	N = 10 36	43
25-49	N = 16 28	60	N = 14 35	51
50-74	N = 18 72	49	N = 13 79	55
75 +	N = 11 57	50	N = 10 60	70
1-49	27	47	35	48
50 +	66	49	71	62
Increase on 1974 1-49 50 +			% 30 8	% 2 27

The trends in these returns can be picked out easily enough. Student numbers in microteaching were expected to rise overall by 15% over the year, but slightly faster where male staff numbers in establishments were higher. The imbalance in the sex-ratios for 1974-5 was in favour of female students where there were fewer male staff (below fifty) but in favour of male students where male staff numbered fifty or more. As shown by the % increases, these ratios narrowed in the returns for 1975-6. For all forty-seven respondents there was near-balance between male and female students. It is as well to recall that the latter outnumbered the former by three to one in the total of teacher training enrolments. We conclude that male dominance was borne out by the data for student involvement in microteaching.

We have shown the connection between numbers of male staff overall, and the numbers of male students in contact with microteaching (table 4.6). As with microteaching activity (table 4.8), the link was more firmly established for local authority colleges in particular. This is so even where *total* student involvement was recorded (table 5.13).

5.13 Students in microteaching in local authority colleges

Male staff in colleges	Average number of students, in micro-teaching 1975-6
1-24	
25-49	35
50 +	87
	177
Average (N = 23)	141

The average number of students for this group of colleges was nearly double that for all other teacher training establishments with microteaching. Two-thirds of the latter reporting had fewer than fifty male staff, contrasting with only one-third of local authority colleges.

The analysis of returns for hours of contact put through microteaching units was limited. The chief obstacle was the way in which respondents used the term 'hours of microteaching'! Here our lack of definition let us down, as some reported hours per student, others the timetabled sessions of teaching. These sessions may have included activities other than the micro-lesson, such as lectures or seminars. In any event, few of the estimates offered would have been accurate, especially where forecasts were made for the year ahead.

For these reasons we laid aside some of the measures used to explore the association of hours of contact with other variables. One example is the numbers of students in microteaching, which would give a prediction of 'out-turn' of units if associated with hours of contact.

The hours of microteaching reported are presented in table 5.14. For the

5.14 Hours of microteaching per session

	1974-5	1975-6	1976-7
	N = 66	N = 49	N = 5
Number of hours	63	73	90
Increase on previous year %	-	16	23
Weighted average of hours	- - - - - - 67 - - - - - 75 - - - - - -
% increase in weighted average	-	11	

year 1974-5 the average of fifty-seven hours gave a ratio of over one hour for every two students. Since forecast increases over the next year were roughly of one quarter (concentrated among respondents in England and Wales), as against 10-15% for student numbers, this ratio would approach one-to-one. As the total of hours estimated for 1974-5 was 3,750 and the student numbers (for the same sixty-six respondents) were 6,550 this ratio of unity seemed fanciful! Estimates for 1975-6 of 3,500 hours and 5,500 students (from fifty respondents) were more subject to statistical variation, yet if they were extended to 1979-80 that 'fanciful' ratio would be achieved.

Microteaching Method

The next part of the survey concerns the methods used to administer microteaching facilities. We designed a frame of responses for the training of staff, as background to similar frames for the tutorial methods employed. By recording respondents' experience in this way we hoped to appraise the quality of teaching on·offer by units.

We show in table 5.15 the pattern of preparation of teaching staff for microteaching activity.

5.15 Staff preparation

Item	Number of responses	% of total responses	% of total respondents (N = 84)
A. Training in skills	35	25	42
B. Discussion in seminars	57	41	68
C. Rating teaching practice	48	34	57
A + B	24		29
B + C	32		38
C + A	17		20
A + B + C	13		15

The mean level of response to single items was 56%, for doubled items it was 33% and for all three as high as 15%, much greater proportions than could be expected by chance. On doubled items one more point will be made; the linking of 'discussion' with 'rating' was significantly greater in statistical terms (to the 1.0% level of confidence) than that of 'training' to 'rating'.

The Tutorial Role in Microteaching

The next section of the survey examined the role of the tutorial in respect of observation, comment and assessment. It is tempting to argue for active and passive roles, but we shall merely indicate items that suggest one or the other.

In asking for information on tutorials we first presented items on the number of students and of tutors involved (table 5.16). Both single and multiple responses were recorded and they are summarized in the form of a simple matrix.

5.16 Tutorials in microteaching

Item	No tutor	Tutor present	Tutor absent or present
	No of responses		No of responses
One student	7	29	5
Student group	13	80	13
One of more students	0	24	2

5.17 Self-evaluation and staff preparation

Item	'Absent tutor' (% of all units responding)
Rating of teaching practice	21
'Training' and 'Discussion'	15

The most common form of tutorial was that of the tutor with a group of students, but that with a single student was operated by one in every three units. The two combined were as frequent as all other paired responses put together.

When the pattern of tutorial practice was compared with staff preparation, we found an association between the 'absent tutor' and the rating of teaching practice by staff.

We examined the extent to which microteaching units used schedules of some kind to record behaviour in the microlesson. Rating was preferred to counting (three times as many responses) and it was the modal item of the multiple responses offered to respondents (table 5.18). Of those *not* using schedules, relatively fewer had reported the training of staff in skills than had reported the other items in preparation of staff. Indeed, 40% of those with staff completing schedules for teaching practice did not use schedules for microteaching practice (the microlesson).

5.18 Use of schedules in microteaching

Item	Number of responses	% of all units N = 84
Rating	43	51
Counting overall	17	20
Counting in sequence	15	18
No schedules	34	40

The assessment of microteaching attracted fewer responses than to the items of 'tutorials' (by 37%) and 'schedules'. This is due to 48% of all units declaring that microteaching was not assessed. This item was, curiously, combined with others in the question (10% of the paired responses), but the most frequent paired response was of staff ratings with student ratings of performance (three in every four pairings). When set against the items on staff preparation, this pairing occurred more often with 'training in skills' (64% of the total response to that item) than with 'rating of teaching' (53%).

This is not a significant difference statistically, but suggests a functional relationship: assessment by rating as a function of staff training.

We have, in tables 5.16 and 5.17, distinguished between present and absent tutors in tutorials. Male staffing does vary for the two sets of responses (table 5.19).

The responses were few enough for differences in financial status to distort the means; local authority colleges used the 'absent tutor' role twice as frequently as did other respondents. We should not ignore the signs of self-evaluation by students, even if the influence of male staffing is discounted.

5.19 Male staffing and tutorial roles in microteaching

Item	Average number of male staff in establishments
Tutor present	44.3
Tutor absent	54.5

We discount this influence on the items on observation; the relatively few respondents using counting schedules were mostly colleges of education. Similar limitations apply to the clear difference (as clear as that in table 5.19) between male staffing by respondents who assessed microteaching assignments and by those who did not. Where differences in male staffing coincided with the most frequent (or modal) responses, its influence has had to be reckoned with, as for the responses on tutorials (table 5.20).

5.20 Male staffing and microteaching schedules

Rating schedules	% of all units	Number of male staff
Rating schedules	51	Average 50.5
Counting or no schedules	26	44.2

The Microclass and Microlesson
In looking at class contact in microteaching, we concentrated on how many of whom are taught in what way and for how long by student teachers.

The make-up of the microclass was highly differentiated. Eighty per cent of the respondents used peer groups of fellow-students, but many used pupils (63%) or both (43%). The average number in a microclass was eight and there was no clear modal value: five or six pupils were as frequent as ten, but two in every three respondents quoted fewer than ten.

If we select those responses for pupils only and for students only, the pattern changes. Class numbers in the former did not differ from the overall, though three in four responses were fewer than ten. Fellow-student classes were larger, averaging over nine, and only half were below ten in number. The two sets of responses together accounted for over half the total of microteaching units (57%).

The microlesson is open to more variation in duration and structure than the class is in composition. We set a limit of thirty minutes to the responses for analysis of time, as lessons of greater length would either have team teaching of some sort or be normal school lessons, and one of ten skills for analysis of practice. Nevertheless, the statistical distribution of lesson times displayed great variation around a mean of over ten minutes, the most frequent value by far. The distribution of skills contained a mean and mode of the same value, six skills. Here the variation was much less, with a standard deviation of roughly half the mean. We looked at the relationship of the microclass to the microlesson and found a value for the correlation of 0.26. The surprising fact is not the magnitude of this value but that it proved positive: larger classes tended to have longer lessons in microteaching.

We found the duration of microlessons associated with both the number of years' experience in microteaching and the range of skills offered in programmes. In broad terms, longer lessons were taught and fewer skills were practised the shorter the period microteaching units had been in operation.

Programmes that began operating prior to 1972 reported microlessons some three minutes shorter on average than those presented in more recent programmes (some three-quarters of the total). They offered in general one more skill than later programmes (seven skills to six) and 23% of them included ten or more skills, against only 13% of the latter. When the two groups of programmes are compared for intensity of microclass contact, there is no difference to be found in terms of minutes' teaching required to work through the range of skills (eighty minutes on average). One difference we noted was in the proportion of microlessons of at least the modal length of ten minutes and of extreme duration: 45% of recent programmes (post-1971) reported the former, compared with 27% of earlier ones, and four of them used lessons longer than thirty minutes (none of the earlier programmes reported such duration).

The estimate of eighty minutes of class contact in the typical microteaching course perhaps needs explaining. If we assume no reteach element in the cycle of skills, then seven skills practised in eleven to twelve minute lessons would give a minimum of eighty minutes' teaching time. For comparison, Ward's recommended programme (1970) of twenty teaching encounters of five minutes' duration would require one hundred minutes to complete, again without the reteach.

We are speaking of the figure for an individual student, but it is possible to apply it to the survey data (table 5.21), and this will be discussed below (p. 66).

5.21 Hours of microteaching

Item	Quantity
Course of 7 skills	80 mins per head
Reteach in three-quarters of courses	60 mins per head
Student numbers, 1975-6	110 per unit
Hours of microteaching approx.	250 per unit per year +
Estimated hours, 1975-6	70 per unit per year

+ $(80 + 60) \times 110 \div 60 = 256.7$

Models in Microteaching

We considered in this section of the survey the use of models. This includes 'model' performance of teaching as well as the cycle of microteaching activities (lessons, lectures, seminars). In table 5.22 we set out responses to the items on films, and then offer detailed analysis in relation to financial status (table 5.23).

5.22 Model lessons in microteaching

Item	Number of responses	% of responses	% respondents
Commercial films	17	14	20
Staff models	33	27	39
Student models	40	32	48
No models	34	27	40
Total	124	100	N = 84

One in four respondents used both staff and student models, and the financial status of these respondents offers unusual evidence of the strength of voluntary colleges in this respect (27% of total).

The clearest impression is of the use of models generated by microteaching units themselves, four times as often as commercial models. University departments preferred their own material only twice as often as they did commercial presentations, but their use of models compared favourably with that of enumerating instruments and of assessment (72% against 47% and 62% of departments respectively).

5.23 The use of models in microteaching and financial status

Item \ Status	Local authority college		Voluntary college		Polytechnic department		University department		Total	
	No	% of total	No	% of total	No	% of total	No	% of total	No	% of total
Staff or student model	34		20		7		12		73	
		47		27		10		16		100
% of total	57		70		70		48		60	
Commercial model	8		2		1		6		17	
		47		12		6		35		100
% of total	13		7		10		24		14	
No model	18		7		2		7		34	
		53		21		6		21		100
% of total	30		23		20		28		27	
Total no	60		29		10		25		124	
		49		23		8		20		100
%	100		100		100		100		100*	

does not add due to rounding

With respect to the elements of microteaching programmes, those of lecture and seminar showed up more clearly in the responses by departments and the 'practical' elements of teach and re-teach more clearly in those by colleges.

The back-up for teaching performance by lectures or seminars could be one advantage of microteaching practice which is rarely found in the school experience.

5.24 Cycles of activity in microteaching

Activity	Number of responses	% of respondents (N = 84)
Teach	62	74
Reteach	48	57
Lecture	38	45
Seminar	58	69
Teach/reteach	40	47
Teach/seminar	29	34
Teach/lecture	26	30
All activities	17	20

5.25 Microteaching activity, financial status and male staffing

Item Status	Teach/reteach	Lecture/seminar
	% of responses	
Colleges	55	45
Departments	48	52
	average number	
Male staff	47.4	44.5

The 'modal' models in microteaching

The patterns of microteaching activity were varied, even within establish-ments, where variation was limited by factors such as size, staff involvement and the date of installation of capacity. Never more than 20% of units reported using all options offered in a question, and two options were the most common response on preparation and participation by staff, observation and evaluation, models and cycles of activity.

There was very little variation by status in responses to each item and.dis-tortion of male staffing levels would be minimal from this factor. The mean levels of male staffing were all within the range of forty-four to forty-six for sets of items, yet the range for single items was thirty-four to fifty-eight male staff.

We stated our intention to describe microteaching practice in terms of the most typical set of responses to certain questions. There are alternatives to this approach, such as the matching of practice to theory in the form of models based on learning theory or to the original techniques of the Stanford model. We summarise the modal responses firstly by listing them by item and to total (table 5.26) and secondly by classifying them according to financial status and identifying the mode for each item and each status (table 5.27). Lastly, we shall examine the group of respondents which operated the most typical microteaching facilities. This group, we shall see, was less usual in other respects, notably in status, in years' experience, and in the range of skills provided for practice by students.

5.26 Items with the highest number of respondents

Item	Number of respondents	% of respondents	Percentage of Items N = 84
1. Discussion in seminars	56	41	67
2. Group tutorials with tutor	80	63	95
3. Rating schedules	43	39	51
4. No assessment	41	32	49
5. Pupils and fellow students	36	43	49
6. Student lessons as models	40	32	48
7. Teach using skills	62	30	74
8. Microteaching in college	79	79	94
9. Microteaching compulsory	55	64	65
Items 2, 3, 4	16	-	19
1, 2, 3, 4	11	-	13
1, 2, 3, 4, 6, 7	7	-	8

It is clear that status is closely linked to the pattern of activity in micro-teaching units. Colleges outnumber departments of education by three to one in the response to the main survey, but by more than this for the modal responses. This applies to the clusters, except for the final group of seven respondents (which includes the unit originating the survey).

5.27 *Financial status and modal responses to items*

Item / Status	College		Department	
	Local authority	Voluntary	University	Polytechnic
	★ indicates most frequent response			
Discuss in seminar Rating schedule	★	•	★	(★)
Tutorial group	•	•	•	•
Rating schedule No schedule	★	★	• •	
Student rating No assessment	★	★	★	(★)
Student models No models	(★)	★	(★)	(★)
Teach Seminar	★	★	(★)	(★)

• indicates response of 50% or more of total for question
(★) indicates margin of one respondent only over other item(s).

If the description of activity in table 5.27 seems selective or even arbitrary, at least it appeared that respondents had a wide enough range of options. They completed over 40% of the total presented, and no full return to the questionnaire was technically possible.

We can offer for comparison the 'modal' model yielded by the survey and the responses that would be appropriate to the Stanford model in its typical form (table 5.28). The key differences that emerge are in the assessment of teaching performance, in the make-up of the microclass and in the range of skills administered.

5.28 Comparison of typical survey responses with the Stanford model

Modal model	Stanford model
Microteach prior to school teaching	⋆
Discussion in staff seminars	⋆
Group tutorials with tutor	⋆
Rating of teaching behaviours	⋆
No assessment of microteaching +	-
Microclass of pupils and of peers	-
Microclass of 5-10 pupils	⋆
Microlesson of 5-10 minutes	⋆
Practice of 6 skills	-
Model student lessons	⋆
Teach / reteach in cycle	⋆
Microteaching in units (not schools)	⋆
Microteaching compulsory	-

+ modal 'pairing' of items was staff/student rating (30% of units)

We continue this account of the survey with a focus on those few respondents who reported almost the entire set of modal items. They displayed some unusual features. For one thing, their microteaching units were well-established, with years' experience more than the average. The modal year of introduction of microteaching (1974), reported by a quarter of all units, was shared by the most typical ones, or the 'magnificent seven' as we might call them.

The fact that none of these units is located in a local authority or university establishment may well have no bearing on microteaching developments of the 'mainstream' variety. We selected three items for a larger sample (of sixteen): group tutorials, rating of behaviour, no assessment of microteaching. All nine of the units additional to the 'seven' were local authority colleges, thus partly restoring the distribution formed by the total of respondents.

The 'modal' models showed a remarkably consistent pattern of class contact and skills content, close to the Stanford model as listed above, but this consistency was not an element in their selection. It was in the composition of the microclass that they were most distinctive. Not one of the group used peers only; school pupils were used relatively more than for respondents as a whole.

The Stanford programme was quoted as a source of microteaching by some 10% of respondents, but not by one of the 'seven'. These, along with other units, used a variety of methods to initiate their programmes, notably courses or conferences at university departments. Most quoted among all units was Stirling University, followed by Lancaster and Liverpool, the 1974 conference at which was the event receiving the most individual mentions.

Definitions of microteaching

We conclude this section of the survey report by going on to discuss the text responses on definitions, objectives and skills in microteaching. These responses formed an impressive array of judgments in areas of interest to practitioners of microteaching. For none of these areas did we offer a model or checklist. In this respect our inquiry differed from the studies reviewed in chapter 3, but it will be brought abreast of these by our presentation and taken beyond them by our concluding discussion, in chapter 8.

If our respondents were taken aback by the absence of a definition of microteaching, they still supplied a gratifying crop of ideas on how to define it. Their definitions did seem related to years' experience of the technique and to the financial status of their institutions. Other likely factors were the available resources, notably the equipment, the microclass and the teaching staff, but we chose not to associate these with the written responses since the task was too daunting and the prospective results too limited.

By employing a 'cut off' for the range of items making up the definition of microteaching (fewer than ten mentions by respondents), we derived nine 'elements' of the method (table 5.29). They were distributed between the different types of establishment, and university departments submitted definitions of a distinct character. Longer in the field than others, these respondents showed a profile that is remarkably smooth, considering the diverse elements involved (figure 5.1a).

The contrast between the highly preferred items and those less preferred than by other respondents is, we think, meaningful; the former group constitutes a somewhat dated description of microteaching and does not refer to the cycle of activity designed to improve the effectiveness of teaching. We have supplied a 'typical' element to maintain the continuum that attractively suggests a functional relationship. Spurious though this may be, it emerges in the response of local authority establishments but with the order of preference reversed (figure 5.1b), since the two sets of responses compete.

The objections to this kind of presentation spring readily to mind. Not only does it involve the relating of samples of widely differing sizes; some 'elements' seem to be re-phrasing of others yet are separated along the continuum. One element is frequently used as a compact definition in itself: the scaled-down encounter. Yet we think that merely counting occurrences is not enough. They should where possible be brought into proportion or into relationship.

Figure
5.1a

The Distribution of Elements in the Definition of Microteaching

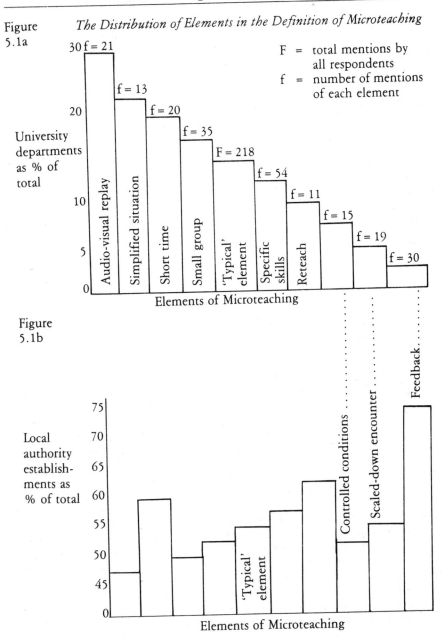

5.29 Elements in the definition of microteaching

Element of microteaching	Number of mentions by respondents			
	LEA/Polytechnics	Voluntary colleges	University departments	Total
Specific skills	32	16	6	54
Small group	19	10	6	35
Feedback	22	7	1	30
Audio-visual replay	10	5	6	21
Short time	10	6	4	20
Scaled down encounter	11	7	1	19
Controlled conditions	8	6	1	15
Simplified situation	8	2	3	13
Reteach	7	3	1	11
Total	88	36	20	144

Considering the elements together, it is clear that most programmes of microteaching in the United Kingdom were conceived in terms of the social psychology of teaching. Learning behaviour was apparently given little regard — much less is known of it for one thing — but in the real classroom situation much more regard has to be given. It may be that a broader conception of teacher-pupil interaction should inform microteaching as it does often the practice of teaching in schools. The next chapter has been designed to enlarge that conception into dimensions rather than sequences of skills.

Further illustration of how microteaching is conceived is provided by statements of objectives, from which the strongest impression is of the dominance of skills, and of the skills themselves (tables 5.30 and 5.31).

Concern with skills accounted for half the statements and with the student as self another quarter, although the table excludes items occurring fewer than six times (some 5% of total mentions). We see this as more of a consensus than a conflict of objectives, and it strengthens the impression gained from Turney (1973).

A less obvious feature of the statements is how they differed by the type of establishment. Applying the Spearman co-efficient of rank correlation, we

5.30 Statements of objectives of microteaching

Objective	Number of mentions by respondents			
	LEA/Polytechnic	Voluntary colleges	University departments	Total
Develop skills	33	14	8	55
Identify skills	13	6	2	21
Self-awareness	7	4	3	14
Self-confidence	7	3	3	13
Self-appraisal	6	3	1	10
Change behaviour	10	0	0	10
Remedial service	3	1	4	8
Initiation	4	1	1	6
Interaction	4	1	1	6
Total	87	33	23	143

obtain a value of + 0.5 for local authority colleges and departments compared with the universities. This corresponds with the value for elements in definitions (table 5.29) and suggests greater convergence than divergence of respondents' views.

The objectives show variation over the full range of classified educational goals in the cognitive domain (Bloom, 1956) and include items in the affective domain. They were shared by all groups of respondents, with the striking exception of the objective 'to change behaviour' of the teacher. Its generality may simply reflect a lack of experience in specifying objectives, but we suspect that the university departments, being more directed toward research and to training courses at higher levels, were registering a lack of interest. They supplied half the statements of the objective 'to apply theory', few as these were, and of that 'to provide a remedial service', so they displayed a practical concern enough. This concern, like that of the colleges, was, not unexpectedly for teacher training institutions, largely with the approach of teachers to classroom activity.

The particular approach of basic skills was clearly dominant in microteaching programmes, and there was substantial agreement among the respondents on the skills presented. The breakdown offered in table 5.32 yields a high rank correlation between universities and other institutions: + 0.93 for the ten most frequently quoted skills, and + 0.85 for the whole series. What differences there existed in the use of skills we show, in table 5.33, in terms of the number of respondents in each of the two groups quoting those skills. Relatively speaking, university departments used least the group of 'managing' skills and the cluster of 'questioning' skills, and they most used some of the skills oriented more towards the learner.

5.31 Analysis of skills employed in microteaching programmes

Skills	Number of mentions by respondents		
	University departments	All other institutions	Total
1. Questioning/redirecting	12	54	66
2. Inducting/initiating/ defining/focussing	10	24	34
3. Reinforcing/encouraging/ praising	11	17	28
4. Closing/recapitulating	8	17	25
5. Varying stimulus	8	16	23
6. Using aids	4	11	15
7. Communicating	4	10	14
8. Presenting/sequencing/ progressing/pacing	2	11	13
9. Participating/using ideas	5	7	12
10. Illustrating/demonstrating	3	9	12
11. Cueing	3	8	11
12. Interacting	3	8	11
13. Expounding/instructing/ narrating	4	5	9
14. Presenting self/poise/ orienting	2	6	8
15. Explaining/elaborating	2	6	8
16. Controlling/manipulating	2	5	7
17. Organizing/planning	1	6	7
18. Discussing	2	4	6
19. Animating/liveliness	3	2	5
20. Structuring/forming concepts	3	1	4
21. Rapport	1	1	2
Total	93	230	323

5.32 Ratio of Responses for Selected Skills

Skill	Mentions by University departments / All other institutions
'Managing':	
Presenting)	
Sequencing)	
Progressing)	
Pacing)	5.7
Organizing)	
Planning)	
'Questioning'	4.5
All skills	2.5 (230 ÷ 93)
Reinforcing	1.5
Participating	1.4

The data on teaching skills can be compared with those produced by Ward (1970) and by Turney (1973) and summarized in chapter 3.

Conclusion
The broad findings are simply stated. Microteaching facilities are widespread among teacher training establishments in the UK. The rate of their installation has probably reached a peak but further provision is to be expected. Operation of the facilities is diversified and small-scale, reaching as yet a small minority of student teachers in training. A typical microteaching unit can be described but its role in practice teaching requires further definition, particularly with respect to assessment of performance.

A great deal of discussion has surrounded the model of microteaching as developed in Stanford University. The model has survived well enough. Our aim was to establish the range and effectiveness of this model, and to this end we did not provide an accepted definition of microteaching. It was important to us to set out the various characteristics of a microteaching facility, so that variations from the typical or the original frame of reference could be detected among respondents. With skills, objectives and research the questions were to be open-ended. A check-list of items was used for the equipment in microteaching.

We had thought of tracing microteaching from its origins, but were reminded that the 'scaled-down teaching encounter' had antecedents. One claimant was that of 'group practice', in the form of several trainees sharing a continuing classroom experience and reviewing events together with their supervisor.

In general, it appears that key members of staff in respect of microteaching found the questionnaire acceptable and the survey appropriate. They seemed interested in seeing a whole picture of microteaching presented so that their own activities could be set in perspective.

The level of expertise and the extent of commitment of resources to micro-teaching we found impressive. The penetration of microteaching into training courses and into establishments was approaching 50%. It was far less than that in respect of student members, perhaps one in six of the 50,000 or so en-rolled in colleges and departments responding to Part II. Proportionately more of the male students and of the higher level courses were located in these active centres.

At the time of survey, the penetration of microteaching into establishments by far exceeded its penetration into the curriculum, whether judged by numbers of students or by hours of contact. Physical expansion of micro-teaching was occurring faster than its development in curricula for the training of teachers. We distinguish two quite distinct scales of operation: one, of up to ninety hours per session, applied to six in every seven units in 1974-5 and the other, of 100 hours or more, applied to the remainder over a considerable range of hours. Quite plausibly the two groups of units operated very different sorts of microteaching activity. Of the 'modal models' drawn out by the survey (p.71), only two were operated on the smaller scale. For this scale the association with student numbers was fairly close, especially in Scot-land and Northern Ireland. This is a guide to quantity in microteaching and also to quality: increasing the hours would usually involve further 'scaling down' of teaching encounters in terms of the skills deployed. In other words, the microteaching programme tends to improve with greater use rather than become 'diluted'.

A second distinction in the data is the regional 'gap' in average hours of microteaching. Scotland and Northern Ireland respondents had roughly three times the number of hours of those in England and Wales in 1974-5. This 'gap' was forecast to narrow slightly over the following year, but the impres-sion again is of distinct scales of operation.

The facts relating to expanding use of microteaching do not give much scope for prediction in terms of hours. If the potential is not limitless it is certainly considerable. The out-turn by hours is influenced by numbers, by equipment, by research inside and outside the units. It is also, we suggest, very much dependent on the extent to which microteaching complements school experience.

The former's contribution of teaching skills is only part of the mesh of social skills formed from actual job experience. Students' evaluation of microteaching will probably never match that of teaching practice. Yet we find the majority of training establishments offering microteaching as a 'gentle introduction' to teaching in classrooms, that is, prior to school experience. This suggests that the 'preparatory' function of microteaching is more often deployed than its 'remedial' function, and that the theoretical content would be the greater where students were being prepared for school teaching than in the post-experience phase of microteaching programmes.

One factor which may have had bearing on the pattern of microteaching activity is its status in the curriculum: whether it is compulsory or optional for student teachers. Some 65% of respondents declared it compulsory, at least for some students and for some hours of contact. Indeed, the average number of hours provided by this group of respondents was seventy. This was exactly 50% more than where microteaching was optional. It would seem a precondition of its being complementary (let alone an alternative) to teaching practice in schools that microteaching experience be required of students. We interpret the substantial majority of programmes organised on this basis as a sign of a reappraisal of school experience in the training of teachers.

We had, perhaps to our shame, already considered how sex-ratios in staffing of establishments might relate to microteaching. In Part I, male staffing was related to other facts. We could, from the main survey, relate it more exclusively to aspects of microteaching activity, such as the role of the tutor.

We regard the quality of staff preparation for microteaching as good. It is quite possible to see the figures in table 5.15 as disappointing, since a number of units seemed not to prepare staff by any of the suggested methods. The single items serve to show that a substantial proportion of respondents prepares staff for microteaching, if only indirectly as with rating of teaching practice. The items selected are not exclusive criteria of preparation, but they seemed familiar to respondents. It is worth recalling that several were at the planning stage and more in the early operating stage of microteaching activity. Again, if we relate preparation to the involvement of staff in microteaching the responses look better. Training in skills, for instance, relates to the use of rating schedules (table 5.18), which received a higher level of response; rating of teaching practice relates to that of students' microlessons (p.66), for which responses were over 40% though at a lower level; more speculatively, discussion in seminars may relate to the use of staff as models (table 5.22), which again earned an activity rate of over 40%.

It is of more interest to us that between one and two-fifths of the respondents combined two of the items, and that one-sixth used all three in preparing staff. Such responses appeared to indicate the variety in methods employed by microteaching units in Britain, and to contribute one of our main objectives: to set out the differences between British 'models' and the Stanford model of microteaching.

We show one such difference in table 5.21 on the hours of microteaching provided for students. Since class contact excludes lectures and seminars by microteaching tutors, there was clearly a shortfall for many students from the reported programme of skills, but for some respondents their data tallied well enough with the out-turn predicted. For instance, the Ulster College cycle generated in 1975-6 some 100 minutes of microclass contact per student; with student numbers of about 260, we would predict around 430 hours of microteaching. The quoted figure for that unit was actually 400 hours. The programmes at Ulster College explore the possibilities of extending the microlesson (chapters 1 and 6), in contrast to the survey findings reported above.

The responses on teaching skills were compared with those on staff preparation (figure 5.2). We noted that discussion in seminars was linked to one or two more skills on average than training in skills and rating of teaching practice. One in three of the respondents quoting this last item declared an 'all or nothing' approach in effect, stating no skills or the whole range of the Stanford model. University units figure least in the responses on skills with no skills specified by one in two respondents, contrasting with one in seven of other units.

The linking of skills to the microlesson should be treated with caution, as one in every five respondents did not declare any skills. With nearly half the respondents quoting fewer than thirty hours' microteaching for 1974-5, this is not so surprising. The practice of specific skills, of impressive number and range, was well-grounded in microteaching units, even where the microlesson was not used. A lesson of normal length could in such cases be used by a group of students deploying different skills in succession on the same topic: a form of team teaching.

Whatever the skills content of the microlesson, there was not a frequent use of instruments for rating or counting teaching behaviours. Users infrequently combined methods of checking on behaviour, namely listing or counting schedules; only one in four used any two of the suggested measures. Since the recording of performance is an invariable feature of microteaching, there would seem to be considerable wastage of material.

We considered the recording of lessons designed as models and whether the training of staff for microteaching may give rise to rejection of the use of recorded models. Returns by local authority colleges showed that their microteaching units

a) trained staff in the use of skills more often — twice as frequently as did others;

b) were as likely to use no model as either staff or student models and this may mean that a form of discrimination training lessons dependence on modelling of skills (Hargie and Maidment, 1978).

There is evidence (McDonald and Allen, 1967; Claus, 1969; Koran et al.,

Figure 5.2a
TEACHING SKILLS AND TRAINING OF
STAFF FOR MICROTEACHING

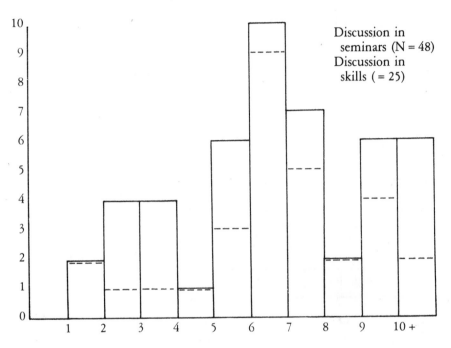

Number of skills in microteaching programme

1969; Borg et al., 1970a) that using models does help the student teacher to learn the behaviours they are designed for. In reviewing their experience of model lessons, Borg and associates doubt that the use of real teachers, situations and lessons is required, and they show convincingly (1970b) that behaviours can change from using models. The problem for operators of microteaching programmes, as Wragg (1974) suggests, is choosing the models to which students are exposed.

These units also favoured the absent tutor and student rating of performance more than other units did. There is only tentative evidence from our survey of withdrawal of tutors from an active or dominant role in microteaching, and we cannot conclude that any withdrawal is associated with recent microteaching development.

Figure 5.2b
TEACHING SKILLS AND STAFF RATING OF
TEACHING PRACTICE (N = 38)

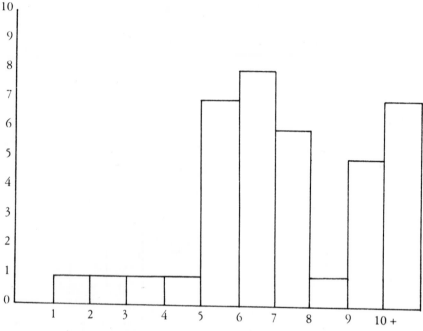

Number of skills in microteaching programme

It seems clear, from the elements of definitions of microteaching (table 5.29 and figure 5.1), that most programmes in the United Kingdom were conceived in terms of the social psychology of teaching. Learning behaviour was apparently given little regard — much less is known of it for one thing — but in the real classroom situation much more regard has to be given. It may be that a broader conception of teacher-pupil interaction should inform microteaching as it does often the practice of teaching in schools.

The social skills model of teaching, which may be likened to the tactical approach stressing components of behaviour outlined by Strasser (1967), has seemingly made a genuine and lasting contribution. Yet, in the form of microteaching, this model has encountered resistance among student teachers and their tutors (see chapter 6).

Some fifteen years after the first application of social skills analysis to a microteaching model, the battery of skills based on motor responses has achieved a considerable extension in teaching methods directed at student teachers. It is now commonplace to observe that 'teaching consists of a variety of skills each of which must be mastered' (Dreeben, 1970) or that 'teaching is a system of action involving (factors) that (the teacher) can modify' (Smith, B O 1963).

We end this presentation and discussion of data gained from Part II of our survey of microteaching by offering a summary (figure 5.3 and table 5.34). This takes the form of a scheme with

1) a core consisting of questions addressed to respondents;
2) items from these questions that represent alternative models of microteaching.

Figure 5.3: *Part II of the questionnaire and 'built-in' models*

Question	Simple Model	Activity	Modal Model
5 Location of micro-teaching in course	after	TEACHING PRACTICE TUTORS	before
8 Preparation of staff for microteaching	teaching practice		staff seminar
9 Staff-student contact	individual	TUTORIAL OBSERVATION	group
10 Instruments of observation	none		rating
11 Assessment		ASSESSMENT	
	none		Staff or students
12 Microclass		CLASS	
	pupils		pupils or peers
19 Location of micro-teaching unit		UNIT	
	school		college
17 Model lessons		MODELLING	
	none		student
18 Cycle of micro-teaching		CYCLE	
	teach		teach and re-teach
20 Attendance at microteaching sessions	optional	ATTENDANCE	compulsory

84 Microteaching in Perspective

*Table 5.33 Summary of questionnaire responses: the 'simple'
and 'modal' models*

	Teaching practice	Tutors	Tutorials	Observation	Assessment
Simple model	25	48	29	34	33
Modal model	70	56	79	43	36

	Microclass	MT Unit	Modelling	Cycle	Attendance
Simple model	25	21	34	62	31
Modal model	·31	79	40	46	55

	Average response (N = 84)
Simple model	34
Modal model	54.5

The 'simple' model is intended to represent not any actual unit but the minimal activity that could be designated as microteaching. The 'modal' model, already examined, approaches the optimum use of resources along the lines of social skills analysis.

We pass on now to a presentation of the problems of and plans for developing microteaching that should indicate why we anticipate interesting new features of the social skills model which informs the microteaching cycle of activity.

Problems, Plans and Microteaching Programmes

We have presented so far, in considerable detail, research findings on and features of microteaching operation. The reader may well have gained the impression that we were engaged in the advertising of margarine, by glowingly picturing the qualities of consistency and smoothness achieved by users of microteaching for research or for teaching.

The Problems of Microteaching
Indeed, our survey did reveal extensive difficulties with the development of the technique of microteaching. Expansion was continuing nonetheless, as shown by the plans being made by respondents, though there were instances of bare survival of programmes and even of termination.

It is not possible properly to account for development of innovations in teacher education particularly because funds are largely provided by local or central government, without pointing to the constraints operating upon them. In the case of microteaching, pressure on resources was the chief, but not the only, friction slowing down progress.

Very few practitioners of microteaching did not acknowledge difficulty, and these failed to specify it more because of its magnitude than of its absence. Of those citing specific problems, a substantial majority (in the sense of a margin over the next group) quoted time as a difficulty. When stated in isolation, 'time' probably represented a number of more definite pressures. Even 'timetabling' was not specific: it could take several forms, and it is worth distinguishing between them.

Pressure on space and on staff, was registered by a sizeable number of establishments, but microteaching had a 'people' problem which was more than that of overwork: one of the 'right' attitudes.

The eight clusters of problems, summarized from some 150 + items (table

6.1), offer comparison with those reported to Turney (1973), not only in their character but in the resistance they collectively present to further development of microteaching. It is this development with which we are especially concerned in this book and the argument we put forward in chapter 7 will require that microteaching go beyond its present limits in application, for us confidently to predict much further penetration by microteaching into teacher education, let alone much improvement in its contribution to effective teaching.

To counter this cautionary note, there is plenty of evidence from our survey that plans were being prepared that would go some way toward relieving difficulties in problems, but first we present the latter in summary form.

6.1 Difficulties encountered in microteaching

Classified items	Number of mentions	%
1. Time + timetabling	60	40
2. Attitudes	25	16
3. Accommodation	18	12
4. Pupils	15	10
5. Equipment	11	7
6. Induction	9	6
7. Technical assistance	8	5
8. Evaluation	7	5
Total	153	100*

* total does not add due to rounding

Since microteaching is a use of educational technology, its greatest problem is the resource base required to carry out programmes. No fewer than four of the clusters in table 6.1 relate to the availability of resources, for which the technique of microteaching has to compete with formidable rivals.

The problem of time is a generic one in education, but it is especially acute in the overcrowded 'traditional' curricula of British teacher training establishments. To us it is clear that rationalization is long overdue, and we offer a **breakdown of the survey items constituting this problem to indicate where it** may be directed:

1. timetabling;
2. staff-student ratio;
3. the microteaching cycle;
4. transportation.

1. Timetabling is an obvious focal point, as there are at least four sorts of timetable involved in a microteaching programme:
   a) the phasing of groups of students through the microteaching units;
   b) the release of students from study in other parts of their course;
   c) the provision of pupils for the microclasses in or from schools;
   d) the other (teaching) duties of microteaching tutors.

We found the difficulty reported by respondents in bringing units 'on line', to cope with the number of students, representing the most frequent single pressure, matching even the vague complaint of 'lack of time'. Not far behind came the ever-present pressure on teaching staff in microteaching units, caused by a complex set of factors. Among these we noted the lack of support by technical and by academic staff, the one because of establishment policy perhaps but the other often simply a matter of attitude.

A second factor was the liaison with schools to fit microteaching programmes in with the normal curriculum. The contacts themselves were sometimes difficult, but more frequently the 'bussing' of pupils to microteaching units or of students to schools was frustrating to the smooth running of units by tutors.

The problem of obtaining pupils has more dimensions than the purely logistical one. It has to be resolved in some way for microteaching to develop satisfactorily, for there seems to be a consensus of opinion that teaching peers is an undesirable departure from the original Stanford model.

The last aspect of timetabling we isolated was the integration of microteaching sessions into the main course of teacher training. The issue is not just one of time; the objection that microteaching is time-consuming may reflect the prevailing priorities in curricula. It is indeed quite practicable to link it with subject specialisms, educational studies and teaching practice and we refer later to plans for integration of one sort or another.

2. One feature of the 'scaled down encounter' is that the ratio of students to staff is also scaled down. The feedback element of the microteaching cycle would seem a highly intensive, if productive, one. In a sector of education where staffing ratios are quite demanding and rigorously scrutinized, the tutorial mode of class contact usual in microteaching has drawn unfavourable comment. There are various ways in which throughput may be increased for programmes but which threaten the benefits to students. One method is to withdraw the reteach from the cycle, and we noted in chapter 5 (table 5.24) that this element was used by little more than half the respondents, several of whom stated that it was omitted under stress to their whole programme. There is some evidence to suggest that this may be a reasonable approach (Clift et al 1976).

3. A third solution relies on the resources of the learner. With careful use of the appropriate rating or enumerating instruments, the microteacher can

acquire the skill of formative self-evaluation or participate in the 'absent tutor' situation with his or her peers. This pattern was reported by few microteaching units (see table 5.16) but we predict the extension of self-evaluation, especially in the light of research findings in this area (Waimon & Ramseyer 1970; Lane 1973; Ellet & Smith 1975). Since microteaching is already an intensive user of capital equipment, it makes sense for units to plan economies in the use of labour.

4. This point applies to the problem of transportation. Whether equipment and microteachers are brought to pupils in schools or the reverse, setting up the microlesson involved waste and risk for the parties concerned. The medium-term solution to this widely reported problem could be, as we will illustrate later in this chapter, to set up microteaching practice much along the lines of conventional school practice. Teams of students were being sent out in this manner of 'block release' at the time of survey, but involvement in the school curriculum remained a difficulty as with school practice.

The second scarce resource was space. This was a problem in both the colleges and the schools, and especially the latter where purpose-built accommodation for microteaching did not exist. From the plans reported to us, we gained the impression that the problem for colleges was largely short term.

This impression extended to difficulties with capital equipment, supplies of which seemed adequate for the most part, though microteaching units did not always have exclusive use of standard television equipment. A more prevalent, if related, condition than shortage, given the reported lack of technical assistance, was the intensity of use, which frequently threatened the standard of service provided by units, such as of recording and replay facilities. We obtained details of the 'hardware' purchased by respondents and present these in Appendix II.

We have already indicated aspects of the problem of making up the microclass. 'Real' pupils gave difficulty even when provided by schools, having met with timetable and transport requirements. The activity in microlessons was felt by some tutors to be too limited for genuine learning behaviours to be observed, since the situation was conspicuously one of practice teaching.

The remaining clusters of problems are more deeply embedded in the nature of the microteaching construct. Evaluation, the least often reported, has been greatly helped by (1) the appearance of a wealth of instruments for the analysis of teaching performance and (2) preparation of staff for microteaching.

One consequence of evaluating students' teaching performance was the pinpointing of weaknesses, which at the least generated anxiety among students. The problem of induction into microteaching centred around the inexperience of students, but even where this was removed by microclass contact there remained, according to some tutors, a sense of threat in the microteaching programme.

We could not explain the incidence of problems relating to attitudes entirely in such terms. Tracing critical attitudes back to root causes is never easy, and a survey questionnaire is far from satisfactory in doing this. Yet the reluctance of some students and staff to accept the technique of microteaching does call for closer inquiry, in our view, especially in the light of the research reviewed in chapter 2. It is a friction on the progress of the technique which can manifest itself in absenteeism (we found attendance optional for a fair number of programmes) and in resistance to a part or to the whole of the cycle of microteaching.

One serious objection was the artificial nature of the practice situation. It was seen as 'mechanistic' in approach because of the stress on skilled behaviours in isolation, as oversimplified in classroom terms and as unrealistic where peers formed the microclass.

Another complaint reported by some staff was against assessment of students' performance, particularly where it contributed to course assessment, although there is evidence to suggest that students actually welcome this (Hargie 1977). We would in such instances suspect the quality of induction into the microteaching set or a paucity of the feedback element in the cycle. The role of the tutor would be open to examination here, as we noted several reports by programme organizers that they lacked support from their colleagues.

The attitude of college and school administrations received scant attention; the issue was clearly stated — the social skills approach was mistrusted by some staff, most of all the breakdown of teaching into its component behaviours. Microteaching experience was not an element in staff promotion or development in the majority of establishments, so few staff were forthcoming in assistance of programmes, even in a research capacity, let alone in respect of modelling or evaluation of teaching behaviour. There were, as we shall illustrate, some hopeful signs of resolving such difficulties; perhaps it was a case of an imperceptible force meeting an improveable object.

Where the 'object' happens to be an institute of education that is a validating body for teacher training courses, the problem of lack of support for microteaching is less tractable. We have already, in chapter 4, indicated areas of relatively little activity and the reader may note significant omissions in the list of 'centre of excellence' quoted as sources of microteaching by respondents (table 6.2).

These sources, were, at the time of survey, still headed by the Stanford University Centre and by one of the early propagators of microteaching in the United Kingdom. There were several means by which the technique was popularized: university conferences, movement of staff pioneering it to other locations, publishing of material and visits to microteaching installations.

Plans for expanding microteaching

It should surprise no one that practitioners of microteaching had a great variety and number of ideas for extending their activities. We have tried to present these in a systematic way, so that some conception may be derived by the reader of how working difficulties were being met at the time of survey.

Such a conception should be aided by the tabulation of problems and plans under a common scheme, once the latter have been set out in some detail

6.2 Sources of microteaching for United Kingdom establishments

University	Number of mentions by respondents
Stanford (USA)	11
Stirling (Scotland)	10
Lancaster (England)	7
Liverpool (England)	6
New University (Northern Ireland)	3
Birmingham (England)	2
Open University (United Kingdom)	1
Total	40

(table 6.3). We prefer a structuring of the analysis, though it requires the use of judgment as to which category a particular item belongs, since our intention is to show where microteaching units are the more likely to develop. This exploration of microteaching activity will be followed by a summary of research, current and planned in 1975, and exemplars of relatively new or unpublicized directions for microteaching.

The classification of plans is somewhat arbitrary, and we have not assigned each problem cited to just one item, though duplicate listing was kept to about 15% of the problems and largely to one of the main classes.

It is clear from the data that respondents were primarily concerned with enlarging the sphere of microteaching activity. Yet, as we showed in table 6.1, there were problems of several kinds reported, and some of these barely related to plans of microteaching units. We particularly noted difficulties requiring schemes of rationalization, and very few plans corresponded to this

6.3 Plans by microteaching units

Class and item	Number of mentions	% of total
Extension of microteaching:	*56*	*67*
1. Hours in operation	4	5
2. Equipment for units	9	11
3. Student groups	5	6
4. Training courses	10	12
5. Skills	6	7
6. School locations	5	6
7. Space for units	6	7
8. Subjects in curriculum	3	4
9. Attendance	2	2
10. Microlesson/microclass	6	7
Operation of microteaching:	*15*	*17*
11. Induction of students/modelling	7	8
12. Staffing	6	7
13. Remedial use	2	2
Integration of microteaching:	*14*	*16*
14. Into courses	2	2
15. With theory	2	2
16. With research	2	2
17. Elements of the cycle/time	7	8
18. Spatial (transporting inputs)	1	1
Total	85	100*

* Total does not add due to rounding

classification (table 6.4). It is mere speculation to suggest that microteaching was still at the quantitative stage of development, for several respondents saw the need for refinement rather than enlargement of facilities, but the data pointed to perhaps twice as much relevance of plans to extension as to operation or to integration of microteaching. It is, after all, easier to get bigger than to get better.

6.4 Problems and plans of microteaching units

Item	Problems		Plans	
	No of mentions	%	No of mentions	%
Extension				
1. Hours in operation	15	10	4	5
2. Equipment	16	11	9	11
3. Student groups	(7)*	(5)*	5	6
4. Training courses	(6)*	(4)*	10	12
5. Skills	(3)*	(2)*	6	7
6. Subject areas	(2)*	(1)*	3	4
7. Space for units	6	4	6	7
8. Attendance	3	2	2	2
9. School locations	9	6	5	6
10. Microlesson/class	6	4	6	7
	65	37	56	67
Operation				
11. Induction/modelling	17	12	7	8
10. Microlesson/class	10	7	(6)*	(7)*
12. Staffing	19	13	6	7
13. Remedial use	5	3	2	2
	51	35	15	17
Integration				
14. Into courses	9	6	2	2
15. With theory	1	1	2	2
16. With research	3	2	2	2
17. Cycle elements	16	11	7	8
18. Spatial/temporal +	12	8	1	1
Total	147	100°	86	100°

+ transport & timetabling
* duplicate listing
° total does not add due to rounding

Even if the licence we have taken, such as in classifying all plans regarding microclass contact as 'extensions' of microteaching, were questioned, the shortfall of plans for operation or integration is marked. There is, however, one type of planning not shown in the tabulations, that of research.

Research into microteaching
Although it was more difficult to classify current ongoing or planned research, of which a proportion was in the nature of ongoing evaluation or design of microteaching experience, some clear impressions did emerge from the survey responses.

There was distinctly less research proceeding or in prospect in England and Wales, compared with Scotland and Northern Ireland. The latter region reported twice the number of specific projects as the former, in proportion to the size of the sample. Again, university departments in England and Wales showed up poorly: only two of these declared research, and a pioneering Scottish department easily exceeded the contributions from those two departments.

The frequency of research was the same, in about one location of microteaching in five for current and for planned activity, but programme evaluation would increase this ratio to perhaps one in three. A popular topic was the relation of microteaching to teaching practice, and modelling also received some attention, along with the integration of microteaching and with the attitudes of staff and students to microteaching. We shall refer to one or two interesting exercises in our concluding chapter because they seem to offer a helpful perspective for the future development of microteaching. This is the justification for our proceeding now to examine a couple of programmes of microteaching currently operating in, as it happens, polytechnic departments.

The School of Education, Newcastle upon Tyne Polytechnic
The microteaching unit at Newcastle Polytechnic began operating only in the 1975-6 session. For us the significant aspect of the venture is the expressed conviction that microteaching activity should serve a worthwhile educational purpose related to the rights and needs of children (Gillam, 1976). For this reason, teaching is organised by pre-service students acting in teams, preferably in the schools, to 'provide a sufficient experience on which work for the children might be based'. The ideal arrangement would be for a period of microteaching practice in schools that assisted the normal preparation of pupils through the curriculum, so that school principals could 'justify the use of "guinea pigs" on educational grounds'.

What interest the Newcastle scheme generates elsewhere should give the opportunity to examine how microteaching complements teaching practice. The two might appear almost indistinguishable but for the planning of microteaching as a course unit. This consists of an induction element, with modelling and discussion, followed by a sequence of lessons, with replay of the feedback on teaching. The microlesson is extended in the later stages, and the unit is completed by feedback on pupil reaction. The course unit takes up a quarter of the practical teaching component in the training curriculum, and is planned for up to 200 students during their second year. We consider that objections as to the scale and to the artificiality of microteaching are met substantially by the Newcastle programme, but much depends upon gaining the co-operation of school staff because of the greater degree of involvement by students in school work.

The School of Communication Studies, Ulster Polytechnic

The prevailing view among microteaching tutors in this School, as with that of Newcastle Polytechnic, is of the critical part played by self-evaluation of students. In this case the students are on a B.Ed training course for secondary teachers, with microteaching treated prior to the first period of school experience. This is in the second year of the course, with a 1977-8 enrolment of eighty students.

The microteaching cycle, without a reteach element, runs through a programme of seven skills, which are partially integrated at predetermined intervals. The student teachers give microlessons in teams to real pupils, until the length of lesson is increased towards the end of the programme. Evaluation is through instruments of ratings used by students themselves, on the basis of written guides and preliminary training. Staff merely act in a supervisory capacity, and the programme has been favourably received by students. (See pages 5-12.)

These brief illustrations of newer perspectives for microteaching bring to a close the presentation of data generated by our survey of 1975. We intend to raise the level of generality of our analysis of microteaching development by examining, in chapter 7, what may lie beyond the application of a social skills model to practical teaching, such as what Strasser calls 'the dimension of the instructional situation'.

The reader should now be sufficiently aware of the research and teaching activity that has been directed at increasing teacher effectiveness through the technique of microteaching. We have ourselves become more aware, through our inquiries, of the limitations and the potentialities of microteaching, and the result has been to explore wider areas of teaching and learning behaviour.

Dimensions of Teaching Behaviour

Introduction: The Social Skills Model
One of the main features of microteaching has been the notion of examining classroom interaction in relation to the behaviour of the teacher and pupils. The rationale behind the simulation of social skills is similar to that which has been adopted for the analysis of motor skills (Argyle 1972). There are certain skills which the good teacher should possess, and so we should train the student teacher to identify and utilize these aspects of teaching behaviour during training. By this method, we are leaving the trainee free to employ whatever teaching skills he wishes in any given teaching situation thereafter. This, briefly, is the rationale behind microteaching, and it is obviously based on behaviourist theory.

Argyle (1972) has, in fact, developed a 'social skills model' based on the model used for the training of motor skills. This social skills model has five central features, namely:-

1. *The aims of skilled performance.* For teachers this includes the transmission of knowledge, information or ideas.

2. *The selective perception of cues.* In the classroom the teacher will receive a number of signals from the class, and the experienced teacher will know how to interpret such signals or cues.

3. *Central translation process.* The brain receives, and deals with, the cues which are perceived from the external world. The actual translation of these cues in the classroom may be conscious. An inexperienced teacher may say to himself: 'This class is getting unruly, what advice have I been given to help me handle such a situation?' With experience such translations become less conscious.

4. *Motor responses.* These are, in effect, the teaching skills prevalent in microteaching. Asking questions, explaining material, using

examples, reinforcing the pupils, varying the stimulus, and so on, are the 'motor responses' which the teacher learns to develop. The pattern of motor responses is characterized by a hierarchical structure beginning with very small, easily identifiable units of behaviour, building up to larger, integrated sequences which comprise these smaller units. Thus, the teacher may begin by administering reinforcement on a fairly mechanical basis (responses such as 'yes': 'that's good') and gradually develop a style of teaching which includes the larger dimension of 'warmth'.

5. *Feedback and corrective action.* The social-skill performer, like the motor-skill performer, uses perceptual cues to correct any mistakes in his performance. Thus the teacher who perceives that the pupils are becoming bored, will immediately attempt to revive interest and motivation by any one of a number of methods.

These five features of the social skills model can be represented diagrammatically as in Figure 7.1.

Figure 7.1 — *The social skills model.*

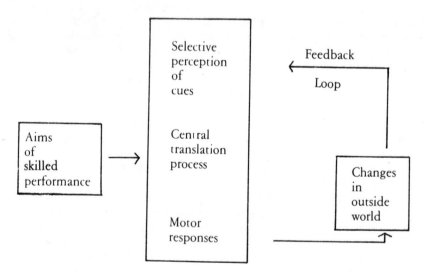

The teacher will observe what effect his motor responses, or teaching skills, have on the class, by observing how the pupils react. This occurs through the selective perception of the cues given by pupils (ie. bored expression, laughter or disbelief). On the basis of this feedback the teacher can, via the central translation process, continue with the same approach or employ a different one. For example, if the experienced teacher begins a lesson by questioning the pupils about what they remember from the previous lesson (motor response), and is faced with either a wall of silence or a series of incorrect responses (observation of changes in outside world) he then becomes aware of this (through feedback and the perception of cues), and decides (central translation process) that he will have to explain once again the information previously covered.

In addition to these five features of the social skills model, there is one other important overall aspect to be considered. This is

6. *The timing of responses.* When a teacher meets a new class for the first time, there occurs a two-way 'feeling-out' process. The teacher will try to convey to the class his expectations and his rules for the future organization of the class. Similarly the class will attempt to ascertain how 'far they can go' with this new teacher — they will test his powers of control. Since the personalities of different teachers and different pupils will vary considerably, this process of 'negotiation' often occurs.

Experienced teachers will have developed techniques which will enable them to cope with such situations — this will be part and parcel of their 'survival kit'. For the trainee teacher, however, the first experience of a new class can range from tense to traumatic. The trainee may be over-friendly at one extreme and find the pupils getting out of control. At the other extreme the trainee may be over-authoritative, causing resentment on the part of the pupils. With reference to the social skills model, it may be that the trainee has not yet developed the full repertoire of relevant motor responses. It may also be that he has not developed the optimal timing for the introduction and variation of these skills.

Microteaching and the Social Skills Model
The above social skills model has, in fact, been the theoretical structure on which microteaching, which is one application of social skills training, has been based. The central focus has been identifying, analyzing, developing and training teachers to utilize the various motor responses or technical skills of teaching, which the teacher uses in the classroom. A number of such component skills have been identified and our survey of the UK revealed a total of at least twenty-one such skills (table 5.32).

A great deal of the literature which has been published in the field of microteaching has indeed emphasized the importance of these. teaching skills as the crucial element in a programme of microteaching. Cooper (1967) expressed the hope that every institution which made use of this technique should attempt to devise, design and evaluate their own specific teaching skills. Meier (1968) and Perlberg (1972) also stressed the importance of these skills, arguing that they increased the choice of behaviours open to trainees; thus individuals became more, rather than less, creative in their teaching.

But many researchers have highlighted other factors involved in a skills approach to teaching. The fact that the original Stanford skills were based on the consensus of opinion of a group of educationists, rather than on more empirical evidence, has caused concern among many researchers. [Sadker & Cooper (1972); McAleese & Unwin (1971); Rosenshine & Furst (1973); Olivero (1970) and Allen & Ryan (1969)]. These are but a few of those who have stressed the need for a systematic evaluation of the reliability and validity of each of the teaching skills which have been introduced. While a certain amount of work has been initiated in order to achieve this objective (see chapter 2), there is a need for more concentrated research in this area.

The Role of the Learner

Another criticism which has been made of the social skills approach to teaching is that it does not consider sufficiently the role of the learner. Social interaction of any kind is, by definition, a two-way process. In short, a lot will depend on the behaviour of all the interactors in any social situation.

From this point of view it can be argued that the social skills model, as applied to microteaching, places the pupil in a passive, recipient role. Brenner et al (1972) in pointing this out, emphasise the need for more consideration of the role of pupils in the teaching process, even in a nonconforming way. This might entail the teacher, for example, discussing his performance with the class, and here it is suggested that microteaching might facilitate such a process. Griffiths (1973) also makes a plea for a more active interpretation of the part played by pupils, and recommends the introduction of more 'global' teaching skills such as 'empathizing' and 'respecting'. This is fact, would fit into the social skills model, whereby these more global motor responses would naturally include and build upon some of the smaller teaching behaviours which are more common in most microteaching programmes.

It may be possible to design a hierarchy of teaching skills. McKnight (1971) suggests classifying the skills of teaching in order of their place in the overall teaching process. Such a task would obviously involve a great degree of research into both microteaching and classroom teaching in order to ascertain whether it is possible to practise all of the elements of teaching in a scaled-down environment. However the development of a hierarchy of such teaching skills would obviate many of the criticisms which have been levelled at microteaching. Although based initially on a behaviouristic rationale the technique would, by evolving the training programme to include dimensions such as warmth, overcome the objection that it focused entirely on small units of teaching, completely out of context. In theory, then, it should be possible to develop microteaching in such a way as to envelop more of the overall teaching strategies and styles, and at the same time place more emphasis on the role of the pupils.

Applying the theory
We have stressed that theoretically it should be possible to enlarge upon the basic social skills model. A number of efforts have already been made in this direction, notably Strasser (1967) and Borg et al (1970a). In addition, some institutions have been concerned with attempts to modify the original Stanford model of microteaching, in a number of ways (see chapter 6). The basic problems are somehow to 'put together again' the act of teaching which has been broken down, and to apply the social skills model to pupils, as well as teachers, in the training programme.

As we have said above, one method of building up the teaching act is to devise a hierarchy of teaching skills, with actual operational behaviours at the bottom, and global teaching approaches at the top. We believe such a device to be possible and suggest a suitable model (figure 7.2). In the case of teacher warmth, we have attempted to illustrate how this global concept could be analyzed in terms of smaller, more easily identifiable skills and behaviours. It has been said, by some behaviourists, that the only way to measure teacher warmth is with a thermometer, but we would disagree!

In our analysis, we divide the teaching dimension of warmth into subdimensions of encouraging, stimulating and relaxing. These are then further divided into skill areas such as 'positive reinforcement', which are in turn presented in terms of sub-skills such as 'nonverbal reinforcement'. Finally these are exemplified in relation to actual observable behaviours, which occur in the classroom.

This model of the teaching dimension warmth is presented merely as one example of how a hierarchy may be formulated. Doubtless the reader will be able to examine other teacher dimensions, such as empathy, in a similar fashion. Indeed the reader may also wish to include other skills or behaviours within the dimension of warmth. As research into classroom dimensions continues (Solomon et al 1964; Haslett 1976) so will it be possible to systematically develop a number of relevant teacher dimensions.

Having formulated a number of hierarchical teaching dimensions, the final step would be to incorporate them into a training programme. This could be achieved by adapting the microteaching format to cater for the dimensional approach. Thus, trainees would be given experience of the lower tiers in our hierarchy (figure 7.2), before moving on to practise elements within the next step. In other words, the trainee would begin at the level of operational behaviours, would then proceed to identify these as sub-skills, skills, subdimensions and, finally, dimensions. In this way, terms such as warmth can

Figure 7.2 — *A hierarchy of skilled performance in the classroom.*

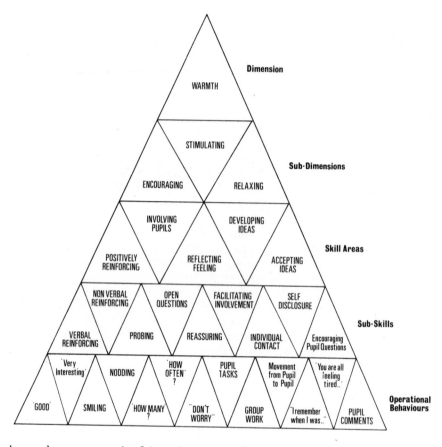

be made more meaningful, and relevant, for the trainee.

It could be argued that this approach represents nothing more than a slight re-structuring and realignment of the teaching skills. The emphasis is still centred on the teacher, with the learner in a subsidiary role. To overcome this objection we must allow the pupils to occupy a more prominent position within the training programme. This could be achieved in a number of ways.

One possibility would be to involve pupils directly in the assessment of student teachers during microteaching. We have already outlined the difficulties involved in this approach (chapter 1), although pupils have proved useful as raters in research studies (chapter 2). To use pupils as a source of feedback would, as Brenner et al (1972) point out, require a less conformist outlook to classroom practice. This outlook might initially meet a fair degree of resistance from many sources.

Perhaps a more immediately applicable method for increasing the role of pupils in microteaching, would be to widen the scope of the teaching skills themselves. This has been attempted in a number of institutions, resulting in the introduction of 'pupil-oriented' skills, such as 'encouraging pupil questions', 'recognizing attending behaviour' and 'use of nonverbal cues to encourage greater pupil participation'. These skills lay stress on the learner being an active, rather than passive, participant in classroom interaction. As microteaching develops and expands, presumably more skills will be outlined in this area, thereby partly overcoming the criticism that the social skills model regards pupils as machines, which can be manipulated at will by the teacher-operator.

The role of pupils could also be increased by integrating microteaching more fully with other course elements. Such teaching modules as 'the psychology (or sociology) of the learner' often occur alongside microteaching, and yet may be regarded as disparate by student teachers. Many of the existing teaching skills (eg. explanation) are dependent on the age and social background of pupils, in that they may require a different focus and presentation, depending on the pupils involved. A number of researchers have highlighted the need for more age, ability and subject specific research, in relation to the validating of teaching skills (Wyckoff, 1973).

Teaching behaviour can be influenced by a large number of factors, any of which may be operative in the classroom at any given time. The sex, age, personalities, social and economic background of the pupils will be directly relevant to the efficacy of the motor responses of the teacher, as may be the subject matter being taught, the time of day or even the behaviour of the teacher in the previous class from which the pupils have come. In relation to the social skills model, these factors form a central element in the feedback loop: indeed, they will have a bearing on the aims of the teacher, as well as his perception of cues, and associated motor responses.

Because the factors we have discussed integrate with the success or failure of the teacher's motor skills, we would argue that they must therefore also be integrated during the training of such motor responses, or teaching skills. But this has not, in fact, usually been the case. Microteaching normally operates largely in isolation from many of the relevant inputs which the trainee receives from other disciplines, such as psychology, sociology and educational studies. The result of this has been that student teachers receive a large number of inputs from a variety of sources, and find it very difficult to relate or integrate these inputs. Naturally students find such a state of affairs unsatisfactory and frustrating, since they have difficulty in ascertaining and evaluating isolated pieces of information. The natural reaction is to question the relevance of each of the academic disciplines to teaching in the classroom. One often hears the age-old joke voiced by students: 'I found my large psychology text book very useful on teaching practice. I used it to hit pupils over the head!'

There may be many reasons why students experience difficulty in applying academic theory to the practical situation. In some instances there may be an element of 'academic snobbery' among sociologists, or psychologists, who value their own subject, but may not feel inclined to apply it specifically to the classroom context (Pond 1977). This raises the issue of 'theory for theory's sake', especially on teacher training courses. We would question the value of pure theory on applied courses, but do not intend to pursue this issue at present, since it is outside the scope of the book.

One other reason for the presentation of certain academic disciplines within teacher education being less than satisfactory, is that no concerted attempt is made to integrate elements of these disciplines in a realistic fashion. Teaching practice is isolated from academic inputs in college. Generalization by trainees from the lecture or seminar, to the classroom, is thus made more difficult.

This would suggest that a two-pronged approach should be developed within teacher education, in order to overcome some of the aforementioned problems. At one level, there should be a greater flow of information between academic disciplines where certain 'themes' may be illustrated by means of information from a number of sources (Wade 1976).

At a second level, some attempt should be made to make theory 'come alive' for students, by highlighting the practical value of the theory itself. It is at this second level that a technique analogous to microteaching would seem to be very useful, where student teachers could experience, in a safe environment, how psychological and socio-economic factors can affect the behaviour of pupils.

Developing the dimensional model

Having formulated a number of global teaching dimensions, which are important in the classroom (ie. warmth, empathy etc), let us now consider how these dimensions affect classroom interaction. It would be useful to develop a model, or structure, to take into account the relevance of these dimensional teaching areas.

If we regard the dimensions as central to teaching, we can then build up a model for classroom interaction, which takes into account most of the factors influencing these dimensions. By developing such a model, the social skills model can be extended considerably while retaining the essential features (perception, motor responses, feedback). The central dimensions will be affected by factors such as personality, age, sex, socio-economic background, needs, values, attitudes of both the teacher and pupils. All of these factors will also affect the selection and employment of motor responses, in any given classroom interaction, by both teacher and pupils. In addition, the perception of cues will be important in relation to the selection of motor skills, the perceptions of both teacher and pupils being dependent in turn upon the 'background' factors (e.g. personality etc). Thus a teacher may feel that he is projecting 'warmth' towards his pupils, but the pupils may perceive the teacher's projection as patronizing behaviour by someone from a different social class, with whom they cannot identify.

Since most of these factors inter-relate in classroom interaction, we decided to illustrate our model by means of a circular flow diagram, which indicates the dynamic nature of the interaction taking place (see figures 7.3 and 7.4). At the centre of this flow diagram are the dimensions of behaviour, and the educational objective concerned. As the flow progresses, these dimensions disseminate gradually through social skills, sub-skills and operational behaviours. At the same time, the teacher and the pupil are represented as poles in the model, which approach one another through stages of classroom interaction or learning activity, that extend as a continuum. The point at which teacher or pupil enters the central area will be representative of the classroom interaction which is taking place.

At one extreme of the continuum the pupil may not recognize even the operational behaviours of the teacher. If this were the case, then mayhem would be the outcome in the classroom. The pupil would not answer questions or follow instructions given as operational behaviours by the teacher. In very few cases would such a situation prevail, although it is not altogether unknown for pandemonium to break loose in classrooms from time to time! A complete break-down of communication, then, is one possibility, and this is clearly represented by our model in figure 7.3.

The other extreme is hopefully more common. At this extreme there is a great deal of concurrence between teacher and pupil, symbolized by dimensions such as warmth, empathy etc. In addition the educational objective of classroom instruction is embraced by teacher and pupil alike (figure 7.4). This is perhaps the ideal teaching situation, and is associated with harmony and enjoyment in the classroom.

In between these two extremes, there is a large number of possible classroom climates. The pupil may, for example, obey instructions and answer questions, while at the same time feeling alienated from the teacher. At a slightly higher level, the pupil may feel pleased when positively reinforced by the teacher, and yet not completely feel at ease in the classroom. These are but a few examples which serve to indicate how our 'dynamic model' of classroom interaction can be applied to many contexts.

At the same time, we would recognize that our model is not without its

Figure 7.3 — *Dimensions of classroom interaction:*
'Non-Response' mode.

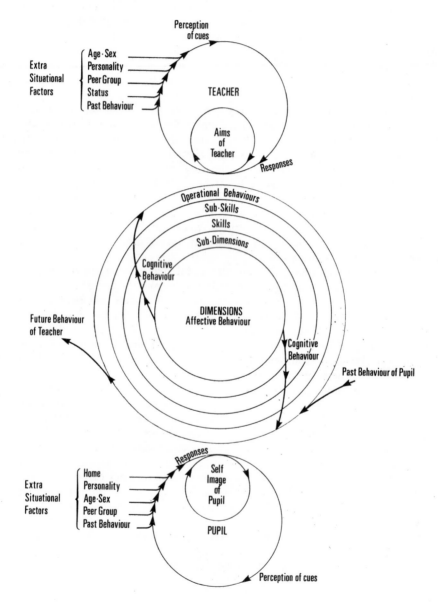

limitations. It does not, for example, illustrate the interchanges between pupils, which are an essential factor in classroom interaction. Instead we have represented interaction as a dyad between instructor and learner. It can readily be seen that a model such as this might usefully be applied to interviewing or counselling contexts, and this in itself has implications for future classroom instruction (see chapter 8). The authors would hope to expand on the development of this model in a later publication, illustrating how it could take into account pupil to pupil interchanges, as well as representing more fully many of the external factors which affect classroom interaction.

The model as it stands does recognize that these inputs exist. Hence factors such as environment, personality and past teaching or learning experiences are fed into the diagram. The aims and self image of teacher and pupil are also recognized, as is the perception of cues through a feedback loop. The two outlets are future teaching behaviour and future pupil behaviour, since these are the immediately recognizable features involved. The process is, by definition an ongoing one. Present experience will be perceived and stored, thereby influencing future behaviour.

Thus the complexities involved in teaching are recognized. Teaching is not just a matter of the teacher behaving in a certain fashion, and the pupil reacting in a predictable manner. But the influence of other factors should not detract from the importance of the skills approach to teaching behaviour. Rather we should concentrate on obtaining more specific information as to exactly how the behaviour of teacher and pupils interact with these other factors. This is one area where educational research may prove to be of value in the future. Keddie (1971) highlights three needs:

'1. To see how the [unequal] distribution of power enters into and shapes the interactional situation in the classroom.

2. To examine the linkages between [what counts as knowledge in] schools and other institutions.

3. To understand the relationship between the social distribution of power and the distribution of knowledge.' (p.156).

In the meantime we would hope that teacher education will develop away from a subject- or discipline-oriented approach, more towards a topic- or theme-oriented approach. To an extent, this has happened within microteaching, in that the technique is one example of an academic discipline being successfully applied. The rationale behind microteaching is based on a theoretical framework derived from the social psychology of group and dyadic interaction, with particular reference to teaching. In this respect many psychologists have demonstrated a willingness to relate theoretical perspectives to practical contexts.

Perhaps we can regard microteaching, or the application of social skills training to teaching, as a starting point upon which we can build. The training of teachers in the use of teaching skills is a worthwhile introduction for students to teaching encounters. We would like to see this extended to include the dimensional teaching areas we have discussed. This would facilitate a 'team' approach by teacher trainers (see examples in chapter 6), whereby knowledge from various disciplines could contribute to the further understanding of the many complexities involved in the classroom.

Figure 7.4 — *Dimensions of Classroom Interaction:* '*Total Response*' *mode.*

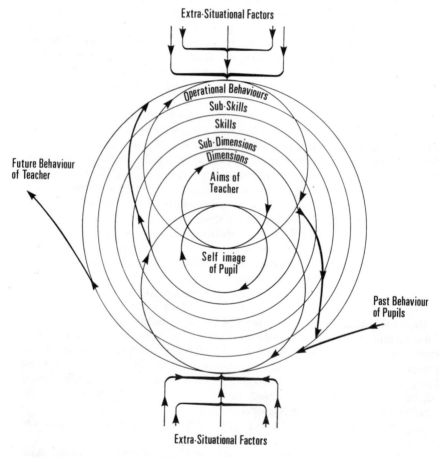

(see Fig. 7.3 for more detail on aspects of the model.)

At present the practical training of teachers consists largely of a high theoretical input coupled with periods of 'apprenticeship' in schools. By initiating a unified programme of teacher training, we could attempt to operationalize and solve many of the problems inherent in teaching, rather than merely illustrating these problems. Instead of discussing possibilities and generalities in teaching, success or failure could be analysed in terms of clearly defined structures or dimensions, and the underlying reasons for the outcome may be more easily determined.

Within such a scheme, the scope and nature of microteaching would be considerably widened. As well as examining the motor responses of both teacher and pupils, the practical exercise could attempt to analyse the various dimensions involved and the factors which operate on these dimensions. This could take place in a simulated situation within the college environment in a manner similar to that employed in traditional microteaching programmes. There would, of course, be differences, as well as similarities to microteaching. It would be desirable to involve pupils from various backgrounds at separate stages, and also to increase the number of pupils and length of lessons. From the point of view of logistics this may be a difficult programme to arrange. It might be possible to arrange with local schools for trainees to visit once each week to teach a practice lesson. A combination of college simulation and classroom practice would be feasible in certain situations.

Regardless of how the programme is initiated, we would recommend that consideration be given to the principles we have outlined. It is not our brief in this book to present a new organizational structure for teacher education, but rather to illustrate how certain avenues may prove more fruitful to explore than others. We would suggest that microteaching has proved to be an efficient method, and that therefore to extend, develop and refine this technique seems a logical path to follow. We have briefly outlined how this might usefully be achieved, and leave the reader to consider our ideas and how they might best be implemented.

The Future of Microteaching

Introduction

Having examined in depth the technique of microteaching and shown it to be both effective and widely used in teacher training, we now intend to turn to the question of what the future holds in store for microteaching both within and without the UK. In order to answer this question we will have to examine microteaching in the general context of teacher education, since changes in the latter will necessitate changes in the former.

It has been argued by Perlberg (1976) that publications in the field of microteaching have decreased in recent years, especially in the American literature. Perlberg reasons that this is because microteaching is no longer an innovation in education, but rather has become a generally acceptable component within teacher training programmes. As a result, educational researchers have moved away from this concept, and are now seeking other methods with which to 'shock the establishment'. In particular, researchers have been advocating reforms in teacher education with emphasis being placed on the notion of 'accountability' in education (Pedersen, 1974).

These arguments are worthy of closer investigation. Perhaps it is true that publications relating to microteaching have declined in recent years, although in order to substantiate such a claim it would be necessary to conduct a comprehensive empirical analysis of the relevant literature. Certainly there would be scope for an up-dated bibliography of microteaching, as a review of some of the references quoted in this book indicates. What does seem to be the case is that, while the concept of microteaching was conceived and initially developed in the USA, researchers in other countries have not been found wanting in producing new ideas in this field.

Our comparison of the surveys of microteaching in various countries (chapter 3) has shown that this is now a widespread method for training teachers. Indeed, although some researchers have moved on to discuss broader issues in education, there is evidence to support the view that educationalists now tend to regard microteaching as an integral part of any teacher education programme. Jensen (1974) illustrates this with reference to the notion of Competency Based Teacher Education. But because some educationalists have chosen to examine wider perspectives, it does not necessarily mean that all researchers will follow suit.

The 'micro' situation is ideal for research programmes. Most of the variables normally prevalent in classroom contexts are reduced, and the remaining variables can be more easily controlled. In addition, the use of videotape recorders means that microlessons can be video-recorded and retained for specific analyses at a later date. This serves to reduce the 'human error' factor in the recording of data, since there is no necessity for instantaneous observation during the actual teaching. Furthermore, there are ample opportunities for researchers in this field to explore, including the following areas:-

1. The efficacy of tutorial feedback.
2. The validity of various teaching skills.
3. The relative effects of different types of audio and/or visual feedback.
4. Types of observation instruments available as a source of feedback.
5. Relationship between microteaching performance and classroom practice.
6. Optimal timing of microlessons.

These, and other variables, were originally outlined by Allen and Ryan (1969) as being in need of closer investigation. While work has already been initiated in a number of these areas, there is much research yet to be conducted. The appeal of the 'micro' context to experimenters in education should encourage the exploration of the various features involved. There is every reason to believe that research projects will continue to further our knowledge of microteaching, in a manner similar to that which has been achieved during the past decade.

Changes in Classroom Teaching

Perhaps at this point it might be useful to briefly reflect on the future of microteaching in conjunction with changes in teacher education. In recent years, there has been a growing feeling of concern that all has not been well in education. Increases in the size of schools, numbers of pupils in classes, and the trend towards violent incidents in classrooms, are central to this feeling of concern. Factors such as these have caused greater problems for teachers than could have been envisaged by even the most pessimistic of educationalists. Many pupils feel alienated in schools, and many teachers find themselves poorly equipped to cope with the resultant attitudes, and behaviours, expressed by pupils.

As a result, developments in education have reflected growing interest in the concept of 'open education'. Turney et al (1976) define open education as being characterized by:

> '...a classroom environment in which there is a minimum of teaching to the class as a whole, and in which provision is made for children to pursue individual interests, to be actively involved with materials and to be trusted to direct many aspects of their own learning. An open classroom thus emphasizes flexibility of curriculum and children's groups, children's decision making, freedom to move about, an atmosphere of trust, acceptance and an honest relationship between teacher and pupils.' (Page 74.)

It can be seen that the central features of such open education are pupil decision-making, involvement and commitment. The teacher in open classrooms plays the role of counsellor, advisor, resource consultant and classroom co-ordinator. As a result the pupil does not perceive the teacher as a disciplinarian whose decisions are to be obeyed upon fear of sanctions. Similarly the job of the teacher becomes a more involved and interesting one, with the major classroom problems of boredom and indiscipline greatly reduced. There are many accounts of open education systems in the literature (Bernstein 1971; Angus 1974). In addition research studies have found open classrooms to be successful (Bussis and Chittenden 1970; Wilson et al 1974). At the same time there is evidence to suggest that not all pupils can cope with, and benefit from open classrooms. Such children, for a variety of reasons, operate at a higher level in traditional classrooms (Ascare and Axelrod 1973; Hampson 1973).

Results such as these seem to indicate a two-tier approach to classroom teaching. For some pupils the open plan classroom will be ideal, providing as it does the freedom for pupils to develop at their own pace. To a certain extent this technique has been applied for many years in Art lessons. What is now being suggested is the extension of open plan to other subject disciplines. The other tier of education will comprise those pupils who cannot function in the open classroom. For these pupils the traditional classroom will be more effective.

Implications for Microteaching

The implementation of a two-tier approach, such as that outlined above, will have implications for microteaching. Teachers in the two types of classroom situation will be required to utilize differing teaching strategies. To a large degree the presently existing set of teaching skills is more applicable to traditional than to open classrooms. The problem facing educationalists would be to identify skills which could be applied in the latter setting. These skills would include behaviours relevant to the teacher in his role as counsellor, advisor, resource consultant, or classroom co-ordinator.

To a certain extent the educationalist can utilize material developed for use in other related fields. A number of counselling skills have already been outlined (Hargie et al 1977a), as have a number of similar skills for those involved in guidance situations (Hargie et al 1977b). Skills such as 'reflection of feeling', 'minimal encourages', 'listening', and 'paraphrasing' would all be of relevance in this context (Ivey 1971). These skills relate to interpersonal behaviour in dyadic situations, and would be of value to the teacher when interacting with individual pupils. In addition the teacher would require organizational and planning skills, as well as managerial and group discussion skills. It is the initiation and development of skills such as these which will probably offer the greatest challenge to future microteaching programmes.

In retrospect it would seem that in many ways microteaching may be regarded as a force within teacher education. Teacher trainers who had become dissatisfied with previous approaches to the practical training of teachers regarded microteaching as a breath of fresh air in the clouded area of effective teaching. With the introduction of microteaching with its associated emphasis on teaching behaviour, educationalists began to examine other wider perspectives in education. As a result there developed movements advocating the total reform and restructuring of teacher education itself.

At the same time, programmes of microteaching have gradually been incorporated into teacher training courses throughout the UK and in many other countries. Trainee acceptance of this technique has been at a high level, despite the finding that there are no significant correlations between a number of personality measures and performance in, or attitude to, microteaching (Austad 1972; Freeman and David 1975; Hargie et al 1977c). This would suggest that, regardless of personality type, students see the relevance of microteaching, and appreciate that it is a practical attempt to overcome some of the problems faced by trainees in the classroom. Given such a finding, coupled with the positive findings relating to the effectiveness of microteaching (chapter 2), it is not surprising that this technique has proved so popular in recent years.

MICROTEACHING IN THE UNITED KINGDOM

The popularity of microteaching in the United Kingdom has been amply demonstrated by the survey presented in chapters 4-6, and we shall conclude our review of the development of the technique by offering for consideration a number of criteria by which the reader may appraise that development. These criteria relate to how far the technique has been adopted and adapted (market penetration and model differentiation) and to how much teaching capacity has been deployed and employed (capitalization and utilization).

1. *The degree of market penetration*
We estimate that microteaching had reached the halfway stage by 1975 in terms of how many of the teacher training establishments were operating or planning facilities. It was only being offered to about 10% of teacher training enrolments, although roughly half of the courses in respondent locations included a microteaching programme.

As the number of enrolments is falling sharply, towards the revised target of only 45,000 places for initial training in 1981, we expect student involvement in microteaching to increase in proportion, if not in absolute terms. There should be a majority of students experiencing the technique by that date, at least of those on in-service courses, long since forecast as the most promising area for this innovation (Allen and Ryan, 1969). In any event, we predict an expansion of microteaching to courses of degree and non-degree level, and an actual rise in the number of locations. This, despite the spate of closures and amalgamations of training establishments, is the likely trend because the method has proved effective and adaptable. If the physical outputs of teacher training are to diminish, their quality should improve. In the economic climate of 1981, whatever it may be, teachers will be entering the occupational structure much better equipped for movement within it than ever before. A higher standard of general education will be combined with a greater range of teaching strategies at the disposal of initiate teachers, but they will also have acquired a competence in social skills that should transfer successfully to other occupations. We may yet see a loss of currency in the term 'microteaching' as the technique becomes one more of 'microtraining'.

2. *The degree of differentiation*
The notion of 'microtraining' is really a culmination of the many modifications that users have brought to bear on the original application of social skills to teaching behaviour known still as the 'Stanford model'. This process of differentiation has been furthered by the growth of research and teaching experience in the United Kingdom's microteaching centres. The 'typical'

model that we presented in chapter 5 may deviate only slightly from the original, but many programmes showed one or more clear departures. These included the extension of microteaching to school locations, the use of self evaluation procedures by students, the lengthening of the microlesson, the partial integration of skills at points during the programme, the abandoning of the reteach element in the microteaching cycle and the location of microteaching with respect to school practice in the training curriculum. Our firm conviction is that, whilst the 'training' element in microteaching may grow, the 'teaching' element will survive. Teacher competence will acquire other aids within the realm of educational technology, but we expect it to derive continuing gains from programmes of microteaching.

3. The degree of capitalization
As an application of technology to education, microteaching has acquired a reputation for effectiveness well-grounded in research. It has, however, given an impression of expensiveness to educational administrators that could be a liability at a time of restraint on public expenditure. This restraint has taken the form of substantial outright cuts in spending in the teacher education sector, as elsewhere in the education system.

Having obtained a considerable amount of information on equipment from our survey, we are able to offer some idea of the capitalization of microteaching. The results are intended to be reassuring that the technique offers good returns on an outlay that, taken in perspective of the lifetime of equipment, is moderate enough for even quite modest programmes of microteaching. The survey returns gave an impression of great variety, a full range and considerable scale of equipment, the cost of which we estimate in broad terms at £½ million. Let us assume at least the same again for accommodation, bringing the total to £1 million. This cost has to be related to rates of depreciation, to hours of operation and to student numbers. Working in very approximate figures of 10% depreciation (over a life-cycle of ten years), 100 students for each of 100 locations and ten hours of microteaching experience per student (over the full cycle of lessons and skills), we derive a capital cost of £1 per student hour (100,000 student hours at £100,000 per annum). The quality of modern equipment is such that this figure will tend to fall even without greater use of facilities.

4. The degree of utilization
We observed from our data that relatively short programmes of microteaching were being offered to a very limited proportion of enrolments in teacher training institutions. Improvements in operation of microteaching units were to be combined with larger numbers of students, with consequent saving of both capital and labour inputs to their programmes. For microteaching to

become even more economical than its high rate of effectiveness suggests, better planning of the use of better equipment by better trained staff would seem essential. Less obviously, we think that fuller integration of micro-teaching into other areas of the curriculum will be required in the longer term.

We intend carefully to examine, in a subsequent book, the question of integration into practical teaching elements of courses and to challenge the self-sufficiency of school practice that until recently had gone for decades without serious question. For the present we have taken up the position that it is not a feasible method of greatly increasing the returns to teacher education. Its direct costs conspire with other factors to make, in our view, capital investment in microteaching installations a much more effective and attractive means of increasing those returns, as a response to the grave doubts expressed by many that teacher education in its present form can meet demands, by government and by society at large, for higher standards of performance in the schooling industry.

In conclusion, we believe that the 'dizzy decade' of microteaching develop-ment in the United Kingdom, from 1966-75, is being succeeded by a 'quiet quinquennium', during which the proportion of training establishments using the method is still rising, if at a slower rate. This continuing build-up of microteaching capacity seems to us sensible in the light of the beneficial effects on the preparation of teachers that have been indicated by our expo-sition of the perspectives of microteaching that has been the central concern of this book.

APPENDIX 1A — Equipment used in Microteaching Units
Number and proportion of locations using

Models	%	1 Camera	2 Lens	3 TV Monitor	4 V/T Recorder	5 Micro-phone	6 Control Panel	Total %
Sony		38	52	49	49	34	21	243
	%	53	58	45	71	51	66	55
Shibaden		21	10	18	7	1	2	59
	%	30	11	17	10	1	6	13
Pye		2	2	17		4	1	26
	%	3	2	16		6	3	6
Philips		3	1	1	1	6		12
	%	4	1	1	1	9		3
Decca		11						11
	%			10				3
National		2	1	1	1	4		9
	%	3	1	1	1	6		2
AKG						9		9
	%					13		2
Ampex			1		7			8
	%		1		10			2
Cannon			8					8
	%		9					2
Akai			3	2	1	1		7
	%		3	2	1	1		2
Cosmicar			5					5
	%		6					1
Other		6	7	9	3	8	8	41
	%	8	8	8	4	12	25	9
Total specified		72	89	109	69	67	32	438
	%	100	100*	100*	100*	100*	100	100
Non-specified		7	27	0	0	13	3	50
All items		79	116	109	69	80	35	488

* percentages do not add due to rounding

APPENDIX IB — Items of Equipment used in Microteaching Units

	1 Camera	2 Lens	3 TV Monitor	4 V/T Recorder	5 Micro-phone	6 Control Panel	Total %
Sony	134	156	287	160	209	40	986
%	61	64	64	70	70	61	66
Shibaden	58	24	59	25	3	6	175
%	26	10	13	11	1	9	12
Pye	2	4	58		16	3	83
%	1	2	13		5	5	6
Philips	9	6	1	6	21		43
%	4	2	0	3	7		3
National	4	3	3	7	11		28
%	2	1	1	3	4		2
Ampex			5	17			22
%			1	7			1
Decca			22				22
%			5				1
AKG					19		19
%					6		1
Cannon		18					18
%		7					1
Cosmicar		16					16
%		7					1
Other	13	16	17	14	22	17	91
%	6	7	4	6	7	26	5
Total specified	220	243	452	229	301	66	1501
%	100	100	100*	100	100	100*	100*
Non-specified	25	91	63	22	55	10	276
All items	245	334	515	251	356	76	1777
%	14	19	29	14	20	4	100

* percentages do not add due to rounding.

APPENDIX IC — Value of Sales of Equipment Used — Microteaching Units

Items of Equipment	Total Number of items	Estimated Cost of all Items £	Approximate Average Cost of Items £
Camera	245	86,000	350
Zoom Lens	167	58,000	350
Fixed Lens	167	2,000	14
TV Monitor	515	58,000	10
V/T Recorder	2515	101,000	400
Video tape	5000	47,000	10
Microphone	356	55,000	155·
Control Panels	76	11,000	150
Intercoms	80	1,000	10
Headphone	177	1,000	7
Portable packs	6	7,000	1,200
Distribution system	1	4,000	4,000
Spotlights	227	4,000	18
Other		4,000	
		439,000	6,600

Average per Microteaching Unit (N = 71)

118

APPENDIX 2: Respondents to the Survey

(Names of establishments as of April 1975)

*Parts I and II of questionnaire returned

Department of Education, University of Wales, Aberystwyth*
Culham College of Education, Abingdon*
Almwich College of Education
Charlotte Mason College, Ambleside*
Normal College of Education, Bangor, North Wales*
St Mary's College, Bangor, North Wales*
Wentworth Castle College, Stainborough, Barnsley
Newton Park College of Education, Bath*
Bath University School of Education
Bedford College of Education*
College of Physical Education, Bedford*
Bingley College of Education*
Bordesley College of Education, Birmingham*
City of Birmingham College of Education*
Newman College, Birmingham
School of Art Education, City of Birmingham Polytechnic*
St Peter's College, Birmingham*
Department of Physical Education, University of Birmingham
Westhill College of Education, Birmingham*
Hockerill College, Bishops Stortford*
College of Education (Technical), Bolton*
Margaret McMillan College of Education, Bradford
Brighton College of Education*
Department of Educational Studies, Brighton Polytechnic*
Department of Art Education, Bristol Polytechnic
Redland College, Bristol
College of St Matthias, Bristol*
School of Education, University of Bristol
Department of Education, Brunel University, Uxbridge*
Caerleon College of Education, Newport*
Hamerton College, Cambridge*
Institute of Education, Cambridge
City of Cardiff College of Education
Llandaff College of Education, Cardiff
School of Art Education, Cardiff College of Art

Welsh College of Music and Drama, Cardiff
Department of Education, University College, Cardiff*
Newland Park College of Education, Chalfont St Giles*
St Mary's College, Cheltenham*
St Paul's College, Cheltenham*
Chester College*
Bishop Otter College, Chichester*
College of Education, Chorley*
St Osyth's College, Clacton-on-Sea
Coventry College of Education*
Crewe and Alsager College of Education
College of Education, Darlington
College of Education, Dartford
Bishop Lonsdale College, Derby
College of.Education, Doncaster*
Nonington College of Physical Education, Dover*
College of Education, Dudley
St Hilda's College, Durham
College of the Venerable Bede, Durham*
Department of Education, University of Durham*
Institute of Education, Durham
College of Education, Eastbourne
Shoreditch College, Egham*
Faculty of Humanities and Education, Middlesex Polytechnic
St Luke's College, Exeter*
School of Education, University of Exeter
Rolle College, Exmouth*
College of Education, Gloucester*
Kesteven College of Education, Grantham*
College of Education, Hereford
Balls Park College of Education, Hertford*
College of Education, Hull*
Endsleigh College of Education, Hull*
Department of Educational Studies, University of Hull*
Borough Road College, Isleworth
College of Education, Ilkley*
Department of Education, University of Keele*
Gipsy Hill College, Kingston-upon-Thames
St Martin's College of Education, Lancaster*
School of Education, University of Lancaster*
Department of Educational Research, University of Lancaster
Department of Educational Studies, Leeds Polytechnic*

All Saint's College, Leeds
Trinity College, Leeds
Department of Education, University of Leeds*
Institute of Education, University of Leeds*
School of Educational Studies, City of Leicester Polytechnic
City of Leicester College of Education*
School of Education, University of Leicester*
Christ's College, Liverpool
City of Liverpool College of Education*
Ethel Wormald College of Education, Liverpool*
F L Calder College of Education, Liverpool*
I M Marsh College of Physical Education, Liverpool*
School of Education, Liverpool Polytechnic*
Institute and School of Education, University of Liverpool*
Battersea College of Education, London
Digby Stuart College, London*
Garnett College, London*
University of London Goldsmith's College
Maria Assumpta College, London
NE London Polytechnic
School of Education, Polytechnic of North London*
Philippa Fawcett College, London*
Rachel McMillan College, London
St Gabriel's College, London
Sidney Webb College, London*
Southlands College, London
Thomas Huxley College, London*
Whitelands College, London*
Institute of Education, London*
King's College, London, Faculty of Education*
Institute of Education, Loughborough*
College of Education, Madeley*
Manchester College of Education
Didsbury College of Education, Manchester*
Elizabeth Gaskell College, Manchester*
Department of Education, Manchester Polytechnic
Department of Audiology, University of Manchester*
College of Education Division, University of Manchester
College of Education, Matlock*
Teesside College of Education, Middlesborough*
College of Education, Milton Keynes*
Faculty of Education, The Polytechnic, Newcastle-upon-Tyne*

Northern Counties College of Education, Newcastle-upon-Tyne*
Institute of Education, University of Newcastle
School of Education, University of Newcastle*
College of Education, Northampton*
Keswick Hall College of Education, Norwich*
Mary Ward College, Nottingham*
School of Education, University of Nottingham
Edge Hill College, Ormskirk*
Lady Spencer-Churchill College, Oxford*
Delegacy for Educational Studies, Oxford*
College of St Mark and St John, Plymouth*
College of Education, Portsmouth*
Poulton-le-Fylde College, Lancs*
Berkshire College of Education, Reading*
School of Education, University of Reading
Eaton Hall College of Education, Retford*
Ripon College of Education*
Lady Mabel College, Rotherham*
College of Education, Saffron Walden*
St Paul's College, Rugby
North Riding College of Education, Scarborough
College of Education, Seaford
City College of Education, Sheffield*
Totley-Thornbridge College of Education, Sheffield*
Department of Education, University of Sheffield*
Radbrook College, Shrewsbury
La Sainte Union College, Southampton*
College of Education, Sunderland
Department of Education, Sunderland Polytechnic*
School of Education, University of Sussex
Anstey College of Physical Education, Sutton Coldfield*
Swansea College of Education
Department of Education, University College of Swansea*
Darlington College of Arts, Totnes
Padgate College, Warrington*
Wall Hall College, Watford*
Faculty of Education, University of Warwick
Weymouth College of Education
King Alfred's College, Winchester*
Teachers' College, Wolverhampton
Technical Teachers' College, Wolverhampton*
College of Education, Worcester*

Cartrefle College, Wrexham*
Department of Education, University of York*
Central School of Speech and Drama, London
School of Theatre, Manchester Polytechnic
Scawsby College of Education, Doncaster
School of Behavioural Sciences, Plymouth Polytechnic*
Brooklands Technical College, Weybridge

Scotland and Northern Ireland
Department of Education, Queen's University, Belfast*
Institute of Education, Queen's University, Belfast*
St Joseph's College of Education, Belfast*
St Mary's College of Education, Belfast*
Stranmillis College of Education, Belfast*
Department of Education, New University of Ulster, Coleraine
Londonderry Technical College*
Department of Communication Studies, Ulster Polytechnic*
Department of Education, University of Aberdeen*
Aberdeen College of Education*
Craigie College of Education, Ayr*
Department of Education, University of Dundee
Dundee College of Education*
Craiglockhart College of Education, Edinburgh*
Moray House College of Education, Edinburgh*
Dunfermline College of Physical Education, Edinburgh*
Callendar Park College of Education, Falkirk*
Department of Education, University of Glasgow
Department of Education, University of Strathclyde, Glasgow
Notre Dame College of Education, Glasgow*
Jordanhill College of Education, Glasgow*
Hamilton College of Education*
Department of Education, University of Stirling*
Department of Education, University of St. Andrews
Department of Education, Heriot Watt University, Edinburgh

Questionnaire

ULSTER COLLEGE
THE NORTHERN IRELAND POLYTECHNIC

Microteaching Unit
Survey of Microteaching in the British Isles

Questionnaire to Educational Establishments:
Part II — Microteaching Aspects*

Q.1   Define briefly what you believe microteaching to be:

_____
_____

Q.2   Which objectives would your microteaching serve?

_____
_____
_____
_____

Q.3   When was microteaching introduced at your establishment?

19...

Q.4   How many of your courses include microteaching?

□ □

124

Q.5 At which stage in your training courses is microteaching *usually* introduced?

Year of course

	1st	2nd	3rd	4th
A. before teaching practice	☐	☐	☐	☐
B. during teaching practice	☐	☐	☐	☐
C. after teaching practice	☐	☐	☐	☐

Please tick only ONE box

Q.6 How many students involved in microteaching?

	Male	Female
A. during 1974-75 session	☐	☐
B. during 1975-76 session	☐	☐

Q.7 How many hours of microteaching in operation?

A. during 1974-75 session ☐

B. during 1975-76 session ☐

Q.8 Do those teaching staff involved in microteaching

please tick

A. receive prior training in behavioural skills? ☐

B. discuss microteaching in staff seminars? ☐

C. complete rating schedules for students on teaching practice? ☐

Q.9 Which form do tutorials in microteaching take?

please tick

A. individual tutorials with one student and one tutor? ☐

B. individual tutorials with one student and no tutor? ☐

C. group tutorials with more than one
student and one tutor? ☐

Ḋ. group tutorials with more than one
student and no tutor? ☐

Q.10 In microteaching tutorials do you use

please tick

A. teaching behaviours listed on rating
schedules? ☐

B. schedules giving total overall counts
of teaching behaviours? ☐

C. a continuous sequence of counts along
a time-line? ☐

D. no observation schedules? ☐

Q.11 In which ways is microteaching assessed?

please tick

A. by staff ratings of students' teaching
performance during microteaching ☐

B. by student's ratings of own teaching
performance during microteaching ☐

C. by completion of assignments relating
to microteaching ☐

D. microteaching is not assessed ☐

Q.12 Who act as pupils in microteaching?

please tick

A. pupils from local schools ☐

B. fellow-students from college courses ☐

C. both school-pupils and fellow-students ☐

Q.13 How many pupils usually comprise a microclass
     in your microteaching?

Q.14 For how long does your *usual* microteaching lesson last?

minutes

Q.15 How many teaching skills are practised in your
     microteaching?
     (Please list below)

_____ _____ _____

_____ _____ _____

_____ _____ _____

Q.16 From which source did you derive microteaching?

please tick

A. from experiences of staff

B. from another educational establishment

Please specify in each case

A. _____

B. _____

Q.17 In relation to the use of model tapes in relation to microteaching, do
you

please tick

A. show commercially available films of
    teaching skills?

B. make your own model tapes using staff
    as models?

C. use good student lessons in microteaching
    as models?

D. not use model tapes at all? ☐

Q.18 Indicate which of the following apply in your microteaching

please tick

A. teach using each of the teaching
skills ☐

B. re-teach using each of the teaching skills ☐

C. related theory lectures on teaching skills ☐

D. related seminars on teaching skills ☐

Q.19 Does microteaching take place

please tick

A. in the training college? ☐

B. in schools? ☐

Q.20 Is microteaching for students ☐

please tick

A. compulsory? ☐

B. optional? ☐

Q.21 What research into microteaching at your establishment is being

A. carried on? _____

_____

B. planned? _____

_____

*Part III of the Questionnaire, which was sent to prospective users of microteaching, differed only
in very slight respects from this Part II Questionnaire.

Bibliography

Ahlbrand, W. P. 'Teacher behavioural cues and student attitude toward the lesson', International MT Symposium, University of Tübingen, West Germany, April 1972.

Allen, D. W., Ryan, K. A. *Microteaching*. Addison-Wesley, 1969.

Allen, W. C. 'An experimental study comparing MT and the traditional method of instruction...', EdD Thesis, East Texas State University, USA, 1972.

Angus, M. 'Opening up Australian primary schools', *New Era, 55* (1974), 90-93.

Argyle, M. *The Psychology of Interpersonal Behaviour*, Penguin, 1972.

Association of Teachers in Colleges and Departments of Education (ATCDE, now NATFHE), *Handbook of Colleges and Departments of Education*, Lund Humphries, 1975, 1976.

Ascare, D., Axelrod, S. 'The use of behaviour modification procedures in four open classrooms', *Psychology in the Schools*, 10 (1972), 243-248.

Austad, C. A. 'Personality co-relates of teacher performance in a micro-teaching laboratory', *Journal of Experimental Education*, 40 (1972), 1-5.

Beattie, N. 'Microteaching — some questions', Edge Hill Forum on Teacher Education, 1, 1 (1972), 80-88.

Bernstein, B. 'Open Schools, Open Society?' in *Class, Codes and Control, Vol. 3*, pp 67-75, Routledge & Kegan Paul, London, 1975.

Bloom, B. S. (ed) *A Taxonomy of Educational Objectives: The Classification of Educational Goals*, Longmans Green, New York, 1956.

Borg, W. R., Kelley, M. L., Langer, P., Gall, M. *The Minicourse: A Microteaching Approach to Teacher Education*, Colier MacMillan, 1970.

Borg, W. R. Langer, P., Kelley, M. L. 'The Mincourse: a new tool for the education of teachers', *Education*, Feb-March (1970), 1-7.

Brenner, I. *et al* 'Aims and developmental procedures for designing teaching stills', International MT Symposium, University of Tübingen, West Germany, April 1972.

Britton, R. J., Leith, G. D. M. 'An experimental evaluation of the effects of MT on teaching performance' in D. Packham, A. Cleery and T. Mayes (eds), *Aspects of Educational Technology*, pp. 262-268, Pitmans, 1971.

Brown, D. P. 'Microteaching and classroom teaching skills', Ed D Thesis, Wayne State University, USA, 1968.

Brown, G. A. *Microteaching: A Programme of Teaching Skills*, Methuen, 1975.

Brown, G. A. 'Using microteaching to train new lecturers', *Educational Media International*, 3 (1976), 12-17.

Brunner, R. 'Microteaching an den Hechschulen der Bundesrepublik Deutschland', *Psychol. im Erzieh. U. Unterr*, 20 Jg (1973), 269-278.

Brusling, C. 'An experiment on MT at the Gothenburg School of Education', University of Gothenburg, Sweden, 1972.

Bush, R. N. 'MT: Controlled practice in the training of teachers', *Communication*, 48 (1966), 201-207.

Bussis, A. M., Chittenden, E. M. 'An analysis of open education', Educational Testing Service, University of Princeton, USA, 1970.

Claus, K. E. 'Effects of modelling and feedback treatments on the development of teachers' questioning skills', *Technical Report No 6*, Stanford Center for Research and Development in Teaching, Stanford University, USA, 1969.

Clift, J. C. *et al* 'A cost effectiveness study of the use of MT in the education of teachers', Report prepared for the Australian Advisory Committee for Research and Development in Education, 1974.

Clift, J. C. *et al* 'The structure of the skill acquisition phase of an MT programme', *British Journal of Educational Psychology*, 46 (2) 1976, 190-198.

Cohen, L. 'Students' perceptions of the school practice period', *Research in Education*, 2 (1969), 52-58.

Collier, K. G. 'The criteria of assessment of practical teaching', *Education for Teaching*, 48 (1959), 36-40.

Coltham, J. 'An experiment in school practice', *Education for Teaching*, 69 (1966), 71-76.

Cope, E. 'Teacher training and school practice', *Educational Research*, 12 (1970), 2.

Cooper, J. M. 'Developing specific skills through MT', *High School Journal*, 51 (1967), 8085.

Davis, R. 'The effectiveness of MT and videotapes in training prospective elementary teachers...', *DAI*, 20 (1970), 4303A.

Delefes, P., Jackson, B. 'Teacher-pupil interaction as a function of location in the classroom', *Psychology in the Schools*, 9, 2 (1972), 119-123.

Dent, H. C. 'An historical perspective' in S. Hewett (ed), *The Training of Teachers: A Factual Survey*, pp. 12-23, University of London Press, 1971.

Department of Education and Science, *Reports on Education*, 1975.

Dreeben, I. C. *The Nature of Teaching: Schools and the Work of Teachers*, Scott Foresman, 1970.

Ellet, L. E., Smith, E. P. 'Improving performance of classroom teachers through videotaping self-evaluation', *Audio-visual Communication Review*, 23. 3 (1975), 277-288.

Emmett, R. *'School practice reappraisal'*, *Times Educational Supplement*, 13 August 1965, 266.

Falus, I. *The Use of Microteaching and Allied Techniques for the Training of Educational Personnel*, United Nations Educational, Scientific and Cultural Organisation, Paris, 1975.

Falus, I., McAleese, W. R. 'A bibliography of microteaching', *Journal of APLET*, 12. 1 (1975), 34-54.

Fortune, J. C., Cooper, J. M. Allen, D. W. 'The Stanford Summer Microteaching Clinic, 1965', *Journal of Teacher Education*, 18 (1967), 384-393.

Freeman, J., Davis, O. L. J. 'Relationships of self-concept and teaching behaviour of secondary teacher candidates in MT', *Contemporary Education*, XLVI, 3 (1975), 215-218.

Fuller, F. F., Manning, B. A. 'Self-confrontation reviewed: a conceptualisation for video playback in teacher education', *Review of Educational Research*. 43 (1973), 469-528.

Gillam, B. C. *Microteaching in Use*, Newcastle-upon-Tyne Polytechnic, England, 1976.

Goldthwaite, D. T. 'A study of MT in the pre-service education of science teachers', DAI, 29 (1969), 3021 A.

Gregory, I. D. 'MT in a pre-service education course for graduates', *British Journal of Educational Technology*, 2, 1 (1971), 24-32.

Griffiths, R. 'The role of the tutor in MT supervision: a survey of research evidence', University

130

of Stirling, Scotland, 1972.

Griffiths, R. 'The future development of MT technique — some possibilities', APLET International Conference on Educational Technology, April, 1973.

Griffiths, R. 'The contribution of feedback to MT technique', APLET/NPLC Conference on Microteaching, January, 1974.

Hampson, E. 'An open-area with staff assistants for special education', The Slow Learning Child, 20 (1973), 52-58.

Hargie, O. D. W. 'An analysis of the reaction of pre-service special education teachers to a programme of MT', Remedial Education, 12. 1 (1977), 22-26.

Hargie, O. D. W., Maidment, P. A. 'Discrimination training and microteaching: implications for teaching practice', British Journal of Educational Technology, 2, 9 (1978), 87-93.

Hargie, O. D. W., Tittmar, H. G., Dickson, D. A. 'Microtraining: a systematic approach to social work practice', Social Work Today 9, 31 (1978), 14-16.

Hargie, O. D. W., Tittmar, H. G., Dickson, D. A. 'Social skills training:applying the concept on a careers guidance course', Bulletin of BPS, 30 (1978), 214-216.

Hargie, O. D. W, Tittmar, H. G., Dickson, D. A. 'Extraversion — Introversion and student attitudes to MT: an empirical analysis', Proceedings of the Irish Educational Studies Conference, University College, Cork, March 1977,84-193.

Haslett, B. J. 'Dimensions of teaching effectiveness: a student perspective', The Journal of Experimental Education, 44, 4 (1976), 4-11.

Health, R. W. Nielson, M. A. 'The research basis for performance-based teacher education', Review of Educational Research, 44 (1974), 463-484.

Ivey, A. Microcounselling: Innovations in Interview Training, C. C. Thomas, Illinois, 1971.

James, P. E. 'Television in teacher training', Visual Education, March (1970), 27-28.

Jensen, L. C., Young, J. I. 'Effect of televised simulated instruction on subsequent teaching', Journal of Educational Psychology, 63, 4(1972), 368-373.

Jensen, R. N. Microteaching: Planning and Implementation a Competency Based Training Programme, C. C. Thomas, Illinois, 1974.

Kallenbach, W., Gall, M. 'MT versus conventional methods of training elementary intern teachers', Journal of Educational Research, 63, 3(1969), 136-141.

Keddie, N. 'Classroom knowledge' in F. D. Young (ed), Knowledge and Control, pp 133-161, Collier-MacMillan, 1971.

Kennedy, K. 'An analysis of the cost of microteaching', Research Intelligence, 2(1975), 54-57.

Kieviet, F. K. 'A Dutch study on MT', International MT Symposium, University of Tübingen, West Germany, April 1972.

Kirwin, N., Shaw, M. 'School and college co-operation on teaching practice', Education for teaching, 70(1966), 44-48.

Kissock, C. 'A Study to test the value of MT in a programme of video-modelling instruction...', PhD Thesis, University of Minnesota, USA, 1971.

Koran, M. L., McDonald, F. J., Snow, R. E. 'The effects of individual differences on observational learning in the acquisition of teaching skill', Annual Conference, American Educational Research Association, 1969.

Kremer, L., Perlberg, G. A. 'The use of MT techniques to train student teachers in stimulating learners' questions', Israel Institute of Technology, 1971.

Lane, C. C. 'Comparative effectiveness of feedback, through videotaping. Purdue teacher evaluation scale and normal supervisory practice, on student teacher attitudes' DAI, 33(1973), 5602 A.

McAleese, W. R. 'MT: a new tool in the training of teachers', Educational Review, 25, 2(1973), 131-142.

McAleese, W. R., Unwin, D. 'A selective survey of MT', Programmed Learning, January (1971), 10-21.

McAleese, W. R., Unwin, D. 'A bibliography of MT', Journal of APLET, 10, 1(1973), 40-54.

131

McDonald, F. J., Allen, D. W. 'Training effects of feedback and modelling procedures on teaching performance', Stanford Centre for Research and Development in Teaching Technical Report No 3, 1967.
McIntyre, D. 'Three approaches to MT: an experimental comparison', Department of Education, University of Stirling, 1971.
McIntyre, D., Duthie, J. 'Student's reactions to MT', Department of Education, University of Stirling, 1974.
McKnight, P.C. 'MT in teacher training: a review of research', Research in Education, 6 November (1971), 24-38.
MacLeod, G. R. 'A study of student self-viewing during MT', University of Stirling, Scotland, 1973.
Meier, J. H. 'Rationale for, and application of MT to improve teaching', Journal of Teacher Education, 19, 2(1968), 145-157.
Moser, C. A., Kalton, G. Survey Methods in Social Investigation, Heinemann, 2nd edn, 1971.
Morrison, A., McIntyre, D. Teachers and Training, Penguin, 2nd edn, 1973.
Nuthall, G. 'A comparison of the use of MT with two types of pupils...', International MT Symposium, University of Tubingen, West Germany, April 1972.
Olivero, J. L. 'The use of video recordings in teacher education', ERIC Microfiche ED 011 074, 1965.
Olivero, J. L. MT: Medium for improving Instruction, Charles E. Merrill Publishing Company, Columbus, Ohio, 1970.
Organization for Economic Co-operation and Development, The International Transfer of MT Programmes for Teacher Education, 1975.
Orme, M. 'The effects of modelling and feedback variables on the acquisition of a complex teaching strategy', PhD Thesis, Stanford University, 1966.

Palmieri, J. C. 'Learning problem children in the open concept classroom', Academic Therapy, 9(1973), 91-97.
Patterson, C. H. Humanistic Education, Prentice-Hall, 1973.
Pedersen, K. G. 'The case for reform in teacher education', Teacher Education, University of Toronto, 7(1975), 4-15.
Perlberg, A. 'Microteaching', International Review of Education, 18, 4(1972), 547-560.
Perlberg, A. 'Microteaching — present and future directions', Education Media International, 2(1976), 13-21.
Perkins, H. V. 'Classroom behaviour and underachievement', American Educational Research Journal, 2(1965).
Perrott, E. 'Course design and MT in the context of teacher training', Paper read at the International MT Symposium, University of Tübingen, West Germany, April 1972.
Perrott, E., Applebee, A., Heap, B., Watson, E. 'Changes in teaching behaviour after completing a self-instructional MT course', Journal of APLET, 12, 6(1975), 348-363.
Perrott, E. et al 'An investigation into teachers' reactions to a self-instructional MT course', Journal of APLET, 13, 2(1976), 25-36.
Peterson, T. 'Microteaching in the preservice education of teachers: time for a re-examination', Journal of Educational Research, 67, 1(1973), 34-37.
Pond, D. A. 'What should we do with applied psychology?' Bulletin of BPS, 30(1977), 13-15.
Price, G. 'Crisis in school practice', Education for Teaching, 65 (1964), 36-40.
Rosenfield, G. W. 'Some effects of reinforcement on achievement and behaviour in a regular classroom', Journal of Educational Psychology, 63, 3(1972), 189-193.
Rosenshine, B. Teaching Behaviours and Student Achievement, IEA Studies No 1 NFER, 1971.
Rosenshine, B., Furst, N. 'The use of direct observation to study teaching' in R. Travers (ed), Second Handbook of Research on Teaching, pp 122-183, Rand McNally, 1973.

Rosenshine, B., Furst, N. 'Research on teacher performance criteria' in B. O. Smith (ed), *Research in Teacher Education: A symposium*, pp 37-72, Prentice-Hall, 1971.

Sadker, M., Cooper, J. 'What do we know about MT', *Educational Leadership*, 29, 6(1972), 547-551.

Selvin, H. C., Stuart, A. 'Data-reading procedures in survey analysis', *American Statistician*, 20, 3(1966), 20-23.

Shepardson, R. 'An analysis of teacher questioning and response behaviours and their influence on student participation during classroom discussions', PhD Thesis, University of Texas, 1972.

Silberman, C. E. *Crisis in the Classroom*, Random House, New York, 1970.

Smith, B. O. 'Toward a theory of teaching' in A. A. Bellack (ed), *Theory and Research in Teaching*, Columbia University, 1963.

Smith, B. O. 'Recent research on teaching: an interpretation', *High School Journal*, 51, 2(1967), 63-74.

Solomon, D., Bezdek, W. E., Rosenberg, L. 'Dimensions of teacher behaviour', *The Journal of Experimental Education*, 33, 1(1964), 23-40.

Spelman, B. J., St John-Brooks, C. 'MT and teacher education. A critical appraisal', *Irish Journal of Teacher Education*, March 1973.

Stones, E., Morris, S. *Teaching Practice: Problems and Perspectives*, Methuen, 1972.

Strasdowsky, R. 'In-service education facilitated by training', PhD Thesis, University of Freiberg, West Germany, 1976.

Strasser, B. 'A conceptual model of instruction', *Journal of Teacher Education*, 18, 1(1967), 63-74.

Tuckman, B., Oliver, W. 'Effectiveness of feedback to teachers as a function of source', *Journal of Education Psychology*, 59, 4(1968), 297-301.

Turney, C., Clift, J. C. Dunkin, K. J., Traill, R. D. *Microteaching: Research, Theory and Practice*, Sydney University Press, Australia, 1973.

Turney, C., Cairns, L. G., Williams, G., Hatton, N., Owens, L. C., *Sydney Micro Skills* (Series 4 Handbook), Sydney University Press, Australia, 1976.

United Nations Economic, Social and Cultural Organisation *New Trends in the Utilization of Educational Technology for Science Education*, UNESCO, 1974, 227-31.

Waimon, M. D., Ramseyer, G. C. 'Effects of video feedback on the ability of evaluate teaching', *Journal of Teachers Education*, 21, 1(1970), 92-95.

Wade, B. 'Initial teacher education and school experience', *Educational Review*, 29, 1(1976), 58-67.

Wagner, A. 'Changing teaching behaviour: a comparison of MT and cognitive discrimination training', *Journal of Educational Psychology*, 64, 3(1973), 299-305.

Ward, B. E. *A Survey of MT in NCATE Accredited Secondary Education Programmes*, Stanford University, USA, 1970.

Wilson, F. S., Stuckey, T., Langevin, R. 'Are pupils in the open plan school different?', *Developing Education*, 2(1974), 28-32.

Wragg, E. C. 'The influence of feedback on teachers' performance', *Educational Research*, June 1971, 217-221.

Wragg, E. C. *Teaching Teaching*, David and Charles, 1974.

Wright, C. 'Report on the use of MT techniques at Hamilton College of Education', MT Conference, Callendar Park College of Education, Scotland, June 1973.

Wright, C. J., Nuthall, G. 'Relationships between teacher behaviours and pupil achievement in three experimental elementary science lessons', *American Educational Research Journal*, 7(1970), 477-493.

Wyckoff, W. L. 'The effect of stimulus variation on learning from lecture', *The Journal of Experimental Education*, 41, 3(1973), 85-90.

Index

Accountability in teacher education, 108
Ahlbrand, W. P., 12, 128
Allen, D., 2, 3, 4, 11, 40, 80, 98, 109, 112, 128
Allen, W. C., 17, 128
Angus, M., 110, 128
Appraisal (see Evaluation),
— of microteaching 4 ff
— of surveys 28 ff
Assessment of school practice, 17 ff
Argyle, M., 95, 128
Ascare, D., 110, 128
Association of Teachers in Colleges and Departments of Education (ATCDE), 42, 49, 128
Attitude
— student, 24
— staff: to microteaching technique, 61 ff
Austad, C. A., 111, 128
Australia
— 1973 survey, 34 ff
Awareness, by colleges of microteaching techniques, 43 ff
Axelrod, S., 110, 128

Beattie, N., 16, 128
Behaviour
— field of, 75 ff
— operationalized, 99 ff

Behavioural approach, 95 ff
Bernstein, B., 110, 128
Bibliography of microteaching, 17
Bloom, B. S., 75, 128
Borg, W. R., 81, 99, 128
Brenner, I., 98, 101, 128
Britton, R., 22, 128
Brown, D. P., 22, 128
Brown, G. 14, 25, 37, 128
Brunner, R., 28, 31, 129
Brusling, C., 11, 23, 129
Bush, R., 5, 22, 129
Bussis, A., 110, 129

Chittenden, E., 110, 129
Claus, K., 80, 129
Clift, J. C., 23, 31, 87, 129
Closure
— of colleges, 42
— as a skill, 3
Cohen, L. 15, 129
Colleges of education or teacher training:
— local authority, 4.1, 4.2
— voluntary, 4.1, 4.2
Collier, K. G., 15, 129
Coltham, J., 16, 129
Competency Based Teacher Education, 109
Computer analysis, 51
Cooper, J., 14, 97, 98, 129, 132

Cope, B., 38, 129
Cost
— capital, 113 ff
— effectiveness, 16
Counselling skills, 111
Criticism
— of microteaching, 16
— of surveys, 28 ff

Davis, O., 111, 129
Davis, R., 21, 24, 129
Definitions of microteaching, 72 ff
Delefes, P., 12, 129
Dent, H. C., 15, 129
Department of Education and Science (DES), 49
Dickson, D. A., 128
Dimensional Model, 99 ff
Discipline
— in class, 95
— as skill, 76
Discrimination
— of skills, 76
— importance of discrimination training, 20 ff
Discussion
— as evaluation of teaching, 16
— as a skill, 76
Dreeben, R. C., 83, 129
Duthie, J., 11, 131

Educational Technology, 113
Effectiveness
— of teaching, 15
— of microteaching, 16 ff
Elements
— of cycle of microteaching, 2ff, 68
— of definition of microteaching, 72 ff
— of 'modal' models in microteaching, 68 ff
Ellet, L., 88, 129
Emmett, R., 16, 129
Empathy, 99
Encouraging, skill of, 99
England and Wales microteaching experience, 52 ff
Enrolment in colleges, 45 ff

Equipment
— cost of, 117
— depreciation of, 113
— items of, 116
Example
— of 'dimensions' in learning, 99 ff
— of microteaching programme, 93 ff
— use of, as a skill, 4
Expansion of microteaching, 112
Experience of microteaching
— by users, 51 ff
— by student, 24
Expertise in microteaching, 54 ff
Explaining as teaching skill, 76

Facilities of microteaching, 61 ff
Falus, H., 17, 28, 31
Feedback
— effectiveness of, 19
— sources of in microteaching, 62 ff
Follow-up
— of microteaching activity, 75
— in survey, 51 ff
Fortune, J., 5, 22, 130
Freeman, J., 111, 129
Fuller, F., 20, 129
Furst, N., 98, 131, 132

Gall, M., 18, 130
Gillam, B., 93, 129
Goldthwaite, D., 5, 18, 129
Gregory, I., 11, 24, 129
Griffiths, R., 11, 98, 129, 130
Group
— practice in teaching, 16
— of teacher training institutions, 118 ff
— teaching 'small groups', 6 ff

Hampson, E., 110, 130
Hargie, O. D. W., 10, 25, 80, 89, 111, 130
Haslett, B., 99, 130
Heath, R., 12, 130
Hierarchy of skilled performance; 100

Institutions of teacher training, 118 ff

Integration
— of microteaching into courses, 71 ff
— of skills, 9
Interaction
— between teacher and pupils, 98
— between pupils, 5
Items
— of equipment, 115
— in questionnaire, 123 ff
Ivey, A., 111, 130

Jackson, P., 12, 129
James, P. E., 10, 130
Jenson, L., 21, 130
Jenson, R. N., 109, 130

Kallenbach, W., 18, 130
Kalton, G., 49, 131
Keddie, N., 105, 130
Kennedy, K., 16, 31, 130
Kieviet, F. K., 11, 130
Kirwin, N., 16, 130
Kissock, C., 17, 130
Koran, M., 80, 130
Kremer, M., 12, 23, 130

Lane, C., 88, 130
Leith, G., 22, 128
Limitations
— to microteaching, 85 ff
— to surveys, 28 ff
Location
— of microteaching units, 52 ff
— of microteaching practice, 83

Maidment, P., 80, 130
Manning, B., 20, 129
Mastering the teaching model, 1 ff
MacLeod, G. R., 11, 131
McAleese, W. R., 1, 11, 17, 98, 130
McDonald, F., 11, 80, 131
McIntyre, D., 11, 23, 131
McKnight, P. C., 1, 11, 98, 131
Meier, J. H., 3, 98, 130
Microclass, 6 ff
Microlesson, 3 ff

Microteaching
— 'absent tutor', 64
— activity, 44 ff
— advantages of, 3
— attitude to, 24
— capitalization of, 113
— concept of, 2 ff
— cycle of, 2 ff, 68
— definition of, 72 ff
— development of, 4 ff
— effectiveness of, 16 ff
— elements in, 69
— equipment for, 116
— feedback, 10
— function of, 75
— hours of contact, 66
— integration into course, 78
— integration of skills, 7, 10
— level of, 44
— lifetime of units, 113
— limitations of, 86
— as 'mechanistic', 98
— microclass, 4 ff
— microlesson, 6 ff
— modelling in, 66 ff
— models of, 70 ff
— objectives of, 75 ff
— on-site location, 85 ff
— operation of, 68 ff
— origins of, 1 ff
— peers in, 5 ff
— planning of, 14
— problems in, 85 ff
— programmes of, 68 ff
— prospects for, 108 ff
— pupils in, 4
— pupil learning in, 7, 25
— as remedial activity, 75
— research in, 16 ff
— resistance to, 86 ff
— resources for, 66
— role of tutor, 10, 62 ff
— self-evaluation in, 10, 62
— skills practised in, 3, 4, 76, 99
— social skills model and, 95, 96
— staffing of, 45 ff

— student numbers, 46, 58-61
— surveys of, 28 ff
— and team-teaching, 7, 93
— as threat to students, 88, 89
— time allocation for, 60
— tutorials, 10, 62
— users in U.K., 118
Microtraining, 112
Model
— microteaching, 66
— 'modal', 68
— social skills, 95, 96
Modelling the master teacher, 1, 2
Morris, S., 1, 3, 29, 132
Morrison, A., 2, 131
Moser, C., 49, 131

Nielson, M., 12, 130
Non-Respondents to survey, 118-122
Northern Ireland, 53, 122
Nuthall, G., 23, 131

Objectives
— of microteaching, 75
— of surveys, 28 ff
Observation, schedules of, 3, 10, 63, 64
OECD, 41
Oliver, W., 11, 132
Olivero, J. L., 11, 98, 130
Open education, 110
Operational behaviours, 99
Orme, M., 11, 131

Palmieri, J. C., 131
Parameters in survey, 42 ff
Patterson, C. H., 131
Pedersen, K. G., 108, 131
Penetration of microteaching
— 'market', 112
— into training courses, 113
Performance
— by students in microteaching, 7, 17 ff
— in teaching, 2 ff, 15 ff
Perkins, H. V., 12, 131
Perlberg, A., 12, 23, 98, 108, 130, 131

Perrott, E., 11, 22, 25, 131
Peterson, T., 18, 131
Polytechnics, 4.1, 4.2
Pond. D. A., 102, 131
Price, G., 16, 131
Priority of skills in microteaching, 76, 77
Problems in microteaching, 85-89
Projection for use of microteaching, 112-114
Prospective microteaching units, 4.3
Public expenditure, 113

Questions
— framing of, 42
— in survey, 123-127
— as teaching skill, 4, 76

Ramseyer, G., 10, 19, 88, 132
Rationale for skills approach, 2, 95, 96
Recipients of questionnaire, 118-122
Recording
— CCTV, 10, 115, 116
— survey data, 42 ff
— units, 91
Relaxing, skill of, 99
Research
— in microteaching, 16 ff
— in teaching, 15
Researchers, assumptions, 28-31
Resources
— financial, 43, 52, 67, 70
— materials, 66
— staff, 57, 61, 64
Reteach in microteaching cycle, 3, 7, 68
Role
— of learner, 98
— of teacher, 98, 99
Rosenfield, G. W., 12, 131
Rosenshine, B., 12, 98, 131, 132
Ryan, K., 2, 3, 4, 40, 98, 109, 112, 128

Sadker, M., 98, 132
Sample, target population of survey, 42
Scale
— of microteaching facilities, 52 ff
— of survey, 42, 43

Scaling-Down of teaching, 3 ff
Schedule (see Observation)
Scotland, 55, 122
Selvin, H., 49, 132
Sex-Ratio in teacher training, 45-48
Shaw, M., 16, 130
Shepardson, R., 12, 132
Silberman, C., 132

Skills
— analysis of teaching, 2 ff, 95 ff
— discrimination of, 19-21
— frequency of in microteaching, 76
— ranking of importance in microteaching, 77
— rating of, 63
Smith, B. O., 16, 83, 132
Smith, E., 88, 129
Social Skills Model
— aims of skilled performance, 95
— limitations of, 97 ff
— and microteaching, 96-99
— motor responses, 95
— translation processes, 95
— selective perception of cues, 95
Solomon, D., 99, 132
Spelman, 16, 132

Staff
— academic, 45, 46, 47, 48, 59, 61
— attitude to microteaching, 85, 89
— induction, 83
— preparation for microteaching, 57, 61, 62
— as resource in microteaching, 71
Stanford University, 1, 2, 3, 4, 90
Status of teacher training institutes, 43, 52
Stimulating, as teaching skill, 99
St. John-Brooks, C., 16, 132
Stones, E., 1, 3, 29, 132
Strasdowsky, R., 56, 132
Strasser, B., 82, 99, 132
Stuart, A., 49, 132
Student
    attitude, 24, 25, 89
    numbers
    — in microteaching programmes, 58, 59
    — in teacher training, 46, 112

Survey
— analysis, 28 ff
— Australia, 34-38
— method, 28-31
— United Kingdom, 39-40, 42 ff
— United States, 31-34
— West Germany, 38-39

'Target' Population, 42-43
Teaching practice
— alternatives to, 16
— assessment of, 15
— effectiveness of, 1, 2, 15
Teaching Skills, 3, 4, 76, 77, 96 ff
Tittmar, H. G., 128
Tuckman, B., 11, 132
Turney, C., 13, 28, 31, 34, 38, 39, 40, 74, 77, 86, 110, 132
'Typical'
— facility in microteaching, 69, 70
— unit of microteaching, 71 ff

Ulster College, 5, 6, 7, 11, 25
UNESCO, 41
Units of microteaching, 48, 52-60
University — Departments of Education, 4.1, 4.2
Unwin, D., 11, 17, 98, 130

Variation
— in microteaching programmes, 57-77
— by region, in microteaching, 5.2
— by status, in microteaching, 5.1

Wade, B., 102, 132
Wagner, A., 11, 18, 132
Waimon, M., 10, 19, 88, 132
Ward, B. E., 14, 65, 77, 132
Warmth, in teaching, 99
West Germany, 38, 39
Wilson, F., 110, 132
Wragg, E. C., 24, 31, 35, 81, 132
Wright, C., 25, 132
Wright, C. J., 12, 132
Wyckoff, W., 13, 26, 101, 132

Young, J., 21, 130